TWAYNE'S WORLD AUTHORS SERIES

A Survey of the World's Literature

Sylvia E. Bowman, Indiana University

GENERAL EDITOR

FRANCE

Maxwell A. Smith, Guerry Professor of French, Emeritus
The University of Chattanooga
Former Visiting Professor in Modern Languages
The Florida State University

EDITOR

Marguerite Duras

(TWAS 147)

TWAYNE'S WORLD AUTHORS SERIES (TWAS)

The purpose of TWAS is to survey the major writers —novelists, dramatists, historians, poets, philosophers, and critics—of the nations of the world. Among the national literatures covered are those of Australia, Canada, China, Eastern Europe, France, Germany, Greece, India, Italy, Japan, Latin America, New Zealand, Poland, Russia, Scandinavia, Spain, and the African nations, as well as Hebrew, Yiddish, and Latin Classical literatures. This survey is complemented by Twayne's United States Authors Series and English Authors Series.

The intent of each volume in these series is to present a critical-analytical study of the works of the writer; to include biographical and historical material that may be necessary for understanding, appreciation, and critical appraisal of the writer and to present all material in clear, concise English—but not to vitiate the scholarly content of the work by doing so.

Marguerite Duras

By ALFRED CISMARU
Texas Tech University

Twayne Publishers, Inc.   ::   New York

This Book Is Dedicated

to

My Parents

ABOUT THE AUTHOR

Professor Alfred Cismaru holds the B.A.
degree from Fordham University and the
M.A. and Ph.D. degrees from New York
University. He has been a teacher of French
and Spanish at 'Brooklyn College in New
York, and he is currently Professor of
French at Texas Tech University, Lubbock,
Texas. His interest in contemporary French
letters has resulted in more than thirty ar-
ticles which have appeared in such scholarly
journals as *The French Review, The Texas
Literary Quarterly, The Antioch Review,
The Kentucky Quarterly* and *The Southern
Humanities Review.* The present study has
been completed after two years of examina-
tion of published and unpublished texts by
Marguerite Duras.

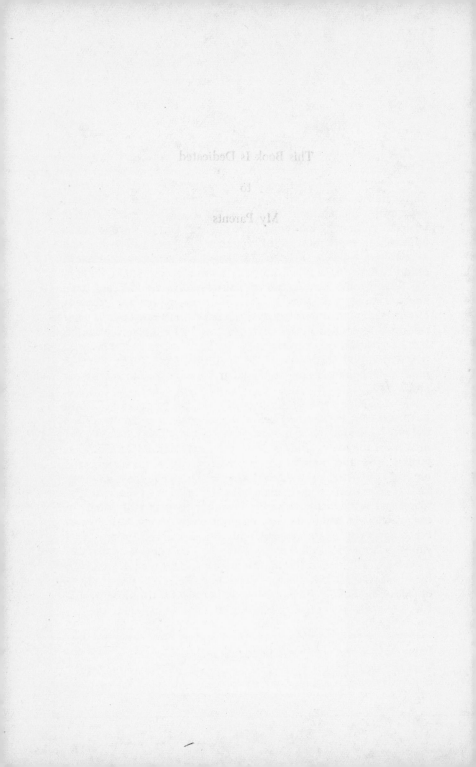

Preface

The purpose of this book is to present to the general reading public and to scholars of present-day literature one of the most noteworthy contemporary French novelists, playwrights, and film writers. Although many of Marguerite Duras' novels have appeared in translation in this country, some are still to become available in English. Most of her plays have not been translated, either here or in England, in spite of the fact that some, notably *Le Square* and *Des Journées entières dans les arbres,* have enjoyed great success in France. It is mostly for the scenario *Hiroshima, mon amour* that Madame Duras attained a considerable reputation in the United States. In France in particular, but in countless other countries as well, the author is gaining in popularity both because of the quality of her work and the number of publications which appear lately at the rate of almost one a year.

The aliterary type of writing penned by Marguerite Duras has been seen by some as belonging to what is generally called the New School, or the Anti-Novel (Anti-Play) School. But in spite of the many affinities with the principles of Alain Robbe-Grillet, Nathalie Sarraute, and other exponents of the group, it is not easy to classify Madame Duras or to categorize, unless it be vaguely and for pedagogic reasons, any one of her works. What makes the task even more difficult is the fact that, owing to the recency of her more famous publications, very few critical comments exist. As the present study is going to press, there is no single volume dedicated to the writer, either here or abroad. This book will, hopefully, fill the lacuna in Durasian scholarship by discussing all her novels, plays, and film scenarios. Because of space limitations, however, and because Marguerite Duras has, at times, reworked a number of titles in different genres, the following exceptions impose themselves: the play versions of *Des Journées entières dans les arbres* and of *Le Square,* the first being only a dramatic reorchestration of the short story, and the second a stage adaptation of the novel; *L'Amante anglaise,* which is a reworking in fiction form of the previously published play,

Les Viaducs de la Seine-et-Oise; Miracle en Alabama, a translation of William Gibron's *The Miracle Worker* which she did in collaboration with Gérard Jarlot and *Détruire dit-elle,* a synthesis of parts of several previous publications.

Because of the unavailability of some novels and plays, and because of the limited circulation of others in this country, it has been deemed necessary to provide the reader, on occasion, with rather detailed summaries and frequent quotations. The latter, always in translation, should make for a more effortless understanding of Marguerite Duras' brilliant themes and preoccupations, which are not always easy to grasp. For the sake of clarity, a division by genre has been adopted: the novels are examined first, followed by a discussion of the plays and of the film scenarios. Since critics have already labeled, somewhat correctly, the early novels as American and the more recent ones as belonging to the New School, one chapter is devoted to those works of fiction which fall within the first category, another to *Les Petits chevaux de Tarquinia* which bridges the two inspirational veins of the writer, and a third to the anti-novels. The text is preceded by an introductory chapter pointing to the advent of French "feminine" writing in our century, and to the special position occupied by Madame Duras on today's literary scene.

Examining the work of a living author is always a delicate undertaking because of the ever-present risk of hurting the sensitivity of the writer or of those closely associated with him. On the other hand, I have been able to uncover only vague and sporadic connections between the literary output of Marguerite Duras and certain events in her life. In general, it did not seem necessary to rely on biographical information in order to explain the author's content or style. Future critics, more removed in time than the present writer, will be able, perhaps, to pinpoint more specifically the relationship which may exist. I see very few now, and none of considerable importance.

Texas Tech University   ALFRED CISMARU

Contents

Contents

Chronology

1914   Marguerite Duras, born April 4 at Giadinh, Indochina, daughter of Henri Donnadieu, professor of mathematics, and of Marie Donnadieu, born Legrand, teacher.

1924   Begins studies at the Lycée de Saigon.

1931   In Paris where she enters the *Faculté de droit* and the *Ecole libre des sciences politiques.*

1935   Obtains her Law degree and a *licence* in political science.

1935   Secretary at the Department of Colonies.

1943   Publishes her first novel, *Les Impudents.*

1944   *La Vie tranquille,* novel.

1950   *Un Barrage contre le Pacifique,* novel; play version by Geneviève Serreau in 1960.

1952   *Le Marin de Gibralter,* novel; movie version in 1966.

1953   *Les Petits Chevaux de Tarquinia,* novel.

1954   *Des Journées entières dans les arbres,* collection of short stories; play version in 1966.

1955   *Le Square,* novel; first play version in 1960.

1958   *Moderato cantabile,* novel; movie version in 1960.

1960   *Les Viaducs de la Seine-et-Oise,* play; *Hiroshima mon Amour,* film scenario; *Dix heures et demie du soir en été,* novel; movie version in 1965.

1961   Collaborates with Gérard Jarlot for the film scenario *Une Aussi lonque absence* which receives the Palm D'Or prize at the Cannes Festival; translates, with Gérard Jarlot, William Gibron's *The Miracle Worker* under the title *Miracle en Alabama.*

1962   *L'Après-midi de Monsieur Andesmas,* novel; collaborates with James Lord for the dramatization of Henry James's *The Beast in the Jungle.*

1963   Conducts interview programs on French television; famous for her probe of the Ben Barka affair that shook France at the time of the Algerian War.

1964   *Le Ravissement de Lol V. Stein,* novel.

1965   Very active in domestic and foreign periodicals, and writing even for such magazines as *Vogue*; *Théâtre I,* containing "Les Eaux et forêts," the definitive play version of *Le Square* and "La Musica."

1966 *Le Vice-Consul,* novel.
1967 *L'Amante anglaise,* novel version of the play *Les Viaducs de la Seine-et-Oise.*
1968 *Théâtre II,* containing *Suzanna Andler,* the printed play version of *Des Journées entières dans les arbres,* "Yes, peut-être," "Le Shaga," and *Un Homme est venu me voir.*
1969 *Détruire dit-elle,* novel.

CHAPTER 1

"Feminine" Literature in France

B EFORE examining the work of Marguerite Duras it is not perhaps unwise to review briefly the tradition of "feminine" writing in France, and the position female novelists occupy in French letters today.

The literary history of no other country is so rich as that of the land of Gaul in remarkable women. Marie de France's reputation for example, has no equal in any other medieval literature. During the Renaissance period, Marguerite de Navarre, sister of King Francis I, published poems and short stories depicting courtly life. In the seventeenth century the Marquise de Lafayette's famous psychological novel, *La Princesse de Clèves* (1678), obtained a well-deserved success and is still read today. Students of French literature and historians marvel at the insight and the informative quality of Madame de Sevigné's letters of the same century. Conspicuously absent from the literary arena of the Age on Enlightenment (women writers are traditionally more concerned with feeling than with thought, and perhaps they could not acquiesce in the trends of readers' taste in the eighteenth century), French female novelists impose themselves in the Romantic era: Madame de Staël's *Delphine* (1803) and *Corinne* (1807) constitute the author's daring defense of the principle of equality of women on the artistic level; George Sand's hundred-odd novels, *Indiana* (1831), *La Mare au diable* (1846), *La Petite Fadette* (1849), and *Histoire de ma vie* (1855), to mention only a few, advocate the end of subjugation of her sex on the social plane and sow, moreover, a greater number of ideas, true and false, in nineteenth-century France, than any other writer's work.

The twentieth century abounds in "feminine" literature, and the novel in particular has witnessed a veritable invasion by women writers. Many Americans have been introduced to the works of Colette, some of which have been transferred to the screen (*Gigi* [1945] for example). Her ability to chisel swift, sensuous sentences, to conjure up the unique taste of tears pour-

ing down a powdered cheek, or the very special feel of male
muscles pressing on a pliant body, marked a skilled workmanship
that has won high praise from French and foreign critics alike.
The mystic Simone Weil and the existentialist Simone de Beauvoir, through their vastly dissimilar work but equally tumultuous
life and through their refusal to submit to a traditional second
place as women or as authors, gave futher impetus to contemporary French fiction before and during World War II.
Françoise Sagan, who has enjoyed (or perhaps suffered from)
the help of Hollywood, is well known in this country for *Bonjour
Tristesse* (1953), *A Certain Smile* (1956), and *Do You Love
Brahms?* (1959). The novels of Françoise Mallet-Joris have not
had the popular success of those of Sagan. But she is a writer's
writer and has obtained much critical acclaim;[1] *Le Rempart des
Béquines* (1951), written at the tender age of nineteen, was
hailed for the revelation it made of the powerful heritage of the
Marquis de Sade; *Les Personnages* (1960) is generally considered to be an admirable historical novel; *Lettre à moi-même*
(1963) is a moving autobiography written with a degree of
sincerity that often makes the reader blush.

But more important than any of the above is Nathalie Sarraute,
the author who, in her book of essays on the novel, *Era of
Suspicion* (1956), explicitly staked out her claim in the field of
writing: the inner, most hidden recesses of the ego, the almost
invisible, amorphous reactions of the self in contact with others,
in the simplest, daily routines. New but infinitely limited—
because of the realm chosen and the vocabulary used, a Sartrian
vocabulary in a non-Sartrian world—Nathalie Sarraute's angry
novels seem to be turning within a rather monotonous circle
appreciated mostly by the literary elite. The inner realm, Sarraute
claims, was only superficially dealt with by Marcel Proust. Her
Portrait of an Unknown (1949), *Martereau* (1953), *Tropisms*
(1957), and *Planetarium* (1959), deal with a petty, middle-class
milieu, where father and daughter; or father, mother, and
daughter; or father, son, and daughter-in-law, live in a kind of
gluelike symbiosis, each suspect, amorphous, inner movement of
the one creating in the others vague, inner retractions, with-
drawals, and conflicts. An eager observer, a young man, watches,
detects, pounces, surmises, weighing the infinitesimal variations
in the climate of each sensibility. He it is who makes the novel
where otherwise there would hardly be a story.

But whether written by Simone de Beauvoir, Sagan, Mallet-Joris, or Sarraute, these are still experimental novels, in both style and technique, still caught in that essential dilemma of the greater novelists of the twentieth century: how to break the closed circle of subjective consciousness, how to create, honestly, a stable, outward reality and, in relation to it, characters with a permanent human identity.

It should be remembered that the political and social structure of postwar France offered a poor background to this need of stability and concreteness. A number of male writers sought refuge in a *littérature engagée,* embracing a cause (communism in the case of Sartre and of the young Camus). In the early 1950s a change of mood among the novelists became evident: Camus broke with Sartre; the aim of the novel did not reside any more in a participation in violent, revolutionary actions seeking to establish a new social order. Camus the Communist became openly what he had really been all along, an artist, a virtuoso (*L'Exil et le royaume* [1951]), and Malraux too, the almost legendary fighter of oriental poverty and capitalism, became the appeased builder of a planetary and Promethean culture (*Le Musée imaginaire de la sculpture mondiale* [1954]) seeking to discover man's inherent but often unknown grandeur.

This more stable though not permanent, outward reality found by the male writers seems to have satisfied but little the rising group of contemporary female novelists. Perhaps because of a difference in temperament, they set out to locate more tangible causes of man's plight in the twentieth century, more immediately satisfying solutions. Their goal was more difficult to attain, and the struggle was further compounded by the necessity of convincing the public to accept their own permanent, human identity and then that of their fictional characters—not an easy accomplishment despite the more and more preponderant role of women in society. Faced with the problem, however, the contemporary French female writers strove, each in her way, to obtain recognition as human beings first, by achieving heights of human endeavor worthy of comparison with those attained by the best male writers: both Simone Weil and Simone de Beauvoir, for example, became doctors and teachers of philosophy, both expounded unpopular social and political views; both traveled, fought, won, and lost battles which dealt always with the major problems of our time. Nathalie Sarraute studied at

Oxford and at the Sorbonne, and received a *licence* in letters and another in law; Marguerite Duras herself is an attorney and holds a *licence* in political science.

Having thus liberated themselves, they proceeded to *free* the others. The angry struggle involved in the attainment of freedom sprang from an almost equal amount of faith in the quality of being a *woman* and of obsessive fanaticism regarding the need for equality. The fight took on the proportions of a crusade; and because like the Crusades it lacked leadership and organization, it was—and is—both successful and abortive, although it does leave the public with an acute sense of urgency for the need to discover a permanent solution concerning woman's place in society and, indirectly, man's position also.

In her two enormous volumes entitled *Le Deuxième Sexe* (1949) and *Mémoires d'une jeune fille rangée* (1958), Simone de Beauvoir poses the fundamental question: What does it mean to be a woman? The books constitute a sincere investigation of the problem. They would impress because of their aggressiveness, were it not that they obtrude because of their notoriety. Simone demands with violence that the injustice which makes Woman an *objet* be immediately stopped. Everything in our society is so ordered, she says, that women, servile creatures, become conscious of their subservience, of the humiliation of being a woman, of the degrading part they must play, often with their consent, in a world where men look upon them as the *enemy,* the *other.* That is to say that once man's conception of woman is changed (if it can be), once he brings himself to regard woman as a fraternal creature, a human being rather than a goddess or an *objet,* then the terrible impasse will cease and woman will have gained her freedom, her happiness.

The situation is not so simple as Simone puts it. First, is it really clear that men are happy (and they ought to be because they are free)? Second, the strength and the influence of the wife in the Scriptures, of the Roman matron who was content to remain home and weave, of most mothers and of all mistresses have, through some miraculous circumstance, attained a degree of expansion, and therefore of freedom, which men often envy and wish they had.

Nevertheless, Simone's anger bore fruit. Her desire for the reincarnation of woman (*objet*-human being) becomes, as we shall see in the course of our analysis of the works of Marguerite

Duras, a need for the reincarnation of both sexes: for man, too, lacks identity and is unable to cope with or recognize a stable, outward reality that could give meaning and reason to his existence.

It should be pointed out, however, that not all contemporary, "feminine" literature is preoccupied with deep psychological or philosophical problems. Intoxicated with their newly acquired freedom, many female novelists have directed their talents to the most profoundly erotic compositions: Christiane Rochefort's *Le Repros du guerrier* (1958), *Judith Albarès* (1958) by Simone Jacquemard, Suzanne Lilar's *Le Divertissement portugais* (1960), the infamous *Histoire d'O* (1961) by Pauline Réage, and the most notorious of them all, *La Bâtarde* (1965) of Violette Leduc, to mention only a few. Their deep involvement in lesbianism, homosexuality, incest, and all sorts of perverted, cerebral, and complicated libidinousness detracts, somewhat from the generally serious tone of more profound writers such as Simone de Beauvoir, Nathalie Sarraute, and Marguerite Duras. On the other hand, the feminine invasion of erotic literature attracts the attention of the public, particularly the male public; and editors, responding, increasingly seek the works of female writers and promote it with the utmost efficiency. Likewise, literary juries, in spite of the often blatantly sensational character of the novels, reward them with prizes that frequently double and triple normal sales. A book such as *Histoire d'O* or *La Bâtarde* helps keep all female novelists in the public eye and further the circulation of the more profound works of better sister authors. The really creative woman thus profits from the ignobleness of less worthy colleagues.

Marguerite Duras, who has never engaged in the writing of scandalous books, plays, or film scenarios, obviously benefited from the favor which contemporary female novelists enjoy. Her career began, inconspicuously enough, during the war period, at a time when the Golden Era of French feminism was in its embryonic stage. Her first novel, *Les Impudents* (1943), and her later *La Vie Tranquille* (1944), did not enjoy great popularity. The author's pen took a long time to mature. The postwar reputation of the American novel prompted many a writer, including Marguerite Duras, to attempt a type of fiction that betrays, like that of other American novelists, the influence of Hemingway: *Un Barrage contre le Pacifique* (1950) and *Le Marin de Gibraltar*

(1952) are notable examples. They are, on balance, passable combinations of adventure, brutality, drunkenness, sexual aggressiveness hiding deep frustrations, and artificial gaiety obscuring poorly the most desolate sadness, loneliness, and boredom.

With *Les Petits chevaux de Tarquinia* (1953), Marguerite Duras moves toward a form which relinquishes the usual supports of fiction writing: the time-space pattern, the development of an action or the presentation of characters. The substance of the story is now hardly definable. The author begins to flirt with the anti-novel,[2] and the relationship between the new genre and the writer will prosper and blossom into the celebrated titles of *Le Square* (1955), *Moderato cantabile* (1958), *Dix heures et demie du soir en été* (1960), and *L'Après-midi de Monsieur Andemas* (1964). However, Duras' present position in the anti-novel school, whose members, incidentally, deny its formal existence, could be the subject of considerable debate. While most of her works since 1953 seem to fall within the general pattern established by such writers as Nathalie Sarraute, Michel Butor, Alain Robbe-Grillet, Samuel Beckett, and others—plotless stories from which motivation, that stock prop of the traditional novel, is patently absent; nameless hero-narrators; banalities expressed by disarming clichés; disregard for psychological verisimilitude; obsessive and contradictory fragments of thoughts and souvenirs; meticulous, precise, and detailed presentation of objects—it is doubtful, as we shall attempt to show, that she has more than an indirect association with the new school. Her stories can, after all, be summarized, and she always manages to evoke a psychological atmosphere, to suggest a human situation, to seize and seal the authentic impasses of heroes and heroines dissatisfied with their condition. As we shall see, there is hope in the novels of Marguerite Duras, and in her plays and movies, too. To be sure, aspirations hardly ever materialize, reincarnation remains utopian when it does not die in embryo, and the essential mediocrity of life becomes ultimately entrenched in the body and soul of most characters. For a moment, though, the hopeful struggle of the attempted metempsychosis has given meaning and reason to one's existence, has reaffirmed the dignity of one's humanity.

The total despair one usually notes in the plays and novels of Samuel Beckett, for example, is absent from the work of Marguerite Duras. But in order to achieve this delicate balance between the lack of a firmly established, friendly reality and

man's need of it, the author had to construct with the greatest
care. The world, such as it is, is unlivable for her characters.
But it is their world, and they will not abdicate until they have
made a number of gestures and have pronounced a number of
words for if they did not make those gestures and did not
pronounce those words we would wonder what else they could
do outside of seeking death by the most expeditious means. The
majority of Marguerite Duras' heroes and heroines will walk
then, will eat and drink, above all drink, and will make love and
go to sleep and wake up and begin again, all the time painfully
aware that victories are gained with the greatest effort, are short-
lived, and always end up in some form of death, physical or
spiritual.

To summarize, then, "feminine" literature is not a modern
phenomenon in France. The creative French woman did not
have to wait for the right to vote or the right to her daily anti-
conception pill in order to make her voice heard. With the exception of the Age of Enlightenment, she contributed through the
centuries to the enrichment of belles-lettres, rivaling at times with
the best of her male counterparts. The recent *benefits* of complete sexual freedom have given rise, in many instances, to a
dubious, if masterful, erotic literature. But a considerable number
of woman writers have resisted the temptation and have pro-
duced highly distinguished works of lasting quality. These works
have portrayed unabashedly the whole of man and woman
engaged in political feuds, in philosophical considerations, in
tender and inimical relationships, with all their loyalty and
infidelity, boredom and solitude, fears and aridity of heart: the
fiction of Simone de Beauvoir, Nathalie Sarraute, and Marguerite
Duras constitutes the most glaring example. These, and similarly
worthy writers, vindicate the expectations of a prophetic vision-
ary whose own proclivities were not directed to the other sex
and who could praise women disinterestedly and reframe them
in his fervid imagination. This foreteller, none other than the
brilliant teenager Arthur Rimbaud, predicted almost a century
ago in his "Seer's Letter":

When the infinite serfdom of woman is broken, when she finally lives
for and by herself, man, hitherto abominable, having then released
her, she too will be a poet. . . . She will discover strange, unfathomable,
repulsive, exquisite things.[3]

CHAPTER 2

The American-Type Novel

I Les Impudents

R ARELY is a first novel a popular success, and *Les Impudents* was no exception. Published in 1943, the author wrote it, for the most part, after the German occupation of Paris when she decided to leave her post as secretary at the Department of Colonies. As it often happens in the case of a living writer, especially of the female sex, there is little biographical data on which to base conclusions. Thus it is that we know nothing of the reasons which prompted Madame Duras to embark upon a career as a novelist. Perhaps the general upsurge of "feminine" literature in France awoke a budding talent, and the fact that she had more free time now favored the painful, solitary struggle of a writer's work.

Les Impudents is not really an American-type novel. Actually, it is difficult to label. It is a beginning, an obscure beginning entirely unnoticed by the wartime literary critics of occupied France. Its tone does not reflect any of the more pressing preoccupations of a war-torn generation, and its characters move in an undated time between World Wars I and II, within a closed circle of subjectivity and egocentricity that recalls the bleak atmosphere of François Mauriac's *Le Noeud de vipères* (1932) and in particular that of his celebrated play, *Les Mal aimés* (1941), which has influenced, perhaps, Marguerite Duras' first attempt at fiction writing. Be this as it may, the public seems to have ignored the book as much as the critics, and were it not for the present fame of the author one would relegate it willingly to oblivion. A first novel is, however, of considerable importance to the literary historian, and merits our detailed consideration here.

Les Impudents is divided in three parts. The first introduces Maud, a twenty-year-old girl; a much older brother, Jacques, whose wife has just died; their mother, Madame Marie Grand-Taneran; a younger stepbrother, Henri; and Maud's stepfather, Mr. Taneran, an inconspicuous person who has given up all attempts at communicating with either his wife or the rest of his family. The love-hate relationship of the Tanerans reminds us of many a family in Mauriac's novels. Jacques had dissipated his money and his wife's dowry in less than a year of marriage, and slyly, unashamedly, he scrounges on what he can get out of his mother and sister. Madame Grand-Taneran is a domineering woman, apparently adoring her sons and daughter but inwardly concerned only with the influence she has on them. Helpful whenever she can be, to just the right degree so that Jacques can continue to come back to her often and maintain his dependence on his mother, Madame Grand-Taneran knows the art of manipulating the beings around her so that her own point of view can always prevail. Henri is first described as a young man who wishes to remain aloof in order to show his scorn for the adopted family of his father, but he winds up imitating Jacques's worldly and rather dishonest ways. Maud alone appears to have genuinely tender feelings for mother and brother, even for Henri and Mr. Taneran. She lends Jacques all the money she can, consoles him on the occasion of the death of his wife, and allows him to cry on her shoulder. Yet, she has no illusions on the inherent selfishness and meanness of her family. It is through her comments, for example, that we become aware of Madame Grand-Taneran's love for power; and after she listens to and comforts Jacques, she feels that "This minute of intimacy with her brother humiliated her as much as a concession she would have made to an enemy."

The enmity of the Tanerans becomes even more predominant in Part II. The family, with the exception of M. Taneran, moves to their estate of Uderan, a farm property they had abandoned for some years, and which is now so uninhabitable that they must seek refuge in the house of a neighbor, the Pecresses. Madame Grand-Taneran's decision was reached in the hope that Jacques's period of mourning would be easier to bear outside of Paris, but she also saw the possibility of her own influence growing unchallenged in the less sophisticated atmosphere of country living. Soon both she and Mme Pecresse discuss the practicality of Maud's marriage with Jean Pecresse, a dull young man for whom Maud feels no attraction at all. But the Tanerans' hosts

are rich peasants, and the Uderan property, ruined as it is, has
no value except to an unwitting buyer. Madame Pecresse is a
shrewd businesswoman: she will buy the Uderan for 50,000
francs, but her son will marry Maud in the bargain, without the
necessity of a dowry, and the Pecresses will thus become tied
with the aristocratic landlords that the Tanerans are. Maud,
aware of the machinations of the two women, would resist, even
if she were in love with Jean, for the fun of opposing her mother
whom she despises more and more. But things become more
complicated when she meets Georges Durieux, a handsome man,
tall, lean and dark in appearance, often riding a horse, and
casting only indifferent looks in the direction of Miss Taneran.
Her love for him stems, initially, from his stubborn and a bit
calculated refusal to court the young girl. She watches him
ignore her and become instead the companion of Jacques, with
whom he often frequents girls and bars. She is suspicious of
Jacques's influence, as well she might be, for on the one hand he
tells Durieux that his sister has been promised to Jean, and on
the other he infers to his mother and Maud that his friend is
an untrustworthy Don Juan who has not the slightest interest in
getting married. This crystallizes Maud's love for Durieux and
her hatred of Jacques, whom her mother defends, in a deft move
to hold on to him at the expense of the daughter.

When the corpse of one of Jacques's girl friends is discovered
by his sister, a sort of complicity develops between her and
Jacques: she will not tell anyone her suspicion that perhaps the
girl had not drowned, as generally believed, that perhaps she
had been pushed into the river; in exchange for her silence,
Jacques will *release* Durieux who, however, persists in ignoring
the girl. But one evening she goes to him with the deliberate
intention of being made love to, of compromising the name of the
family to which she belongs, in particular the undeserved respectability of her mother and her plans to trade her to the
Pecresses. "I came to you because I had enough," she says to
him. "Today again they've been unbearable."

When mother and brother discover what they consider to be
the treason on her part, she is content to live in the house of
Durieux, as his mistress, and to vegetate during the day, waiting
for him to return from his walks, his riding and hunting, in order
to find a moment of pleasure in his arms at night. Durieux does
not appear to love Maud at all, or perhaps he leaves her so often

alone in order to give her a chance to think things over, to be very sure that the path she has chosen is the best under the circumstances. She will not tell him that she is pregnant and, proud, she will accompany her mother and Jacques back to Paris rather than force Durieux into a marriage he might later regret. Madame Grand-Taneran, on her part, will become reconciled with her daughter after selling Uderan to the Pecresses. She knows fully well that Jean will marry her although he is aware of her stay in Durieux's house. She imagines that Maud must have had enough of her lover by now, and she comments: "Actually I found him too old for you. I also wanted to tell you that here no one knows that you stayed at his place. You did not go out with him, you were prudent, that's very good. . . . The Pecresses, who know everything, kept quiet. You will learn to know them, they are decent people."

In Part III, however, serious complications set in. The obvious pregnancy of Maud precludes the possibility of marriage to Jean. In fairness to all concerned Madame Grand-Taneran is bound to return the 50,000 francs to the Pecresses, and to cancel the arrangement. But Jacques had made considerable debts, he had borrowed money from a loan company which threatens to have him arrested for failure to meet payments, and the police had come to look for him in their Paris apartment. Maud knows that her mother will eventually use the money to bail Jacques out. It is then that her own hatred takes shape, that it ceases to be dormant or patient and it seizes upon the occasion in order to commit that one act which will make her position unequivocally clear to others and to herself: her own hostility springs forth, unashamed and liberating the moment she finds herself in the anteroom of a police station, facing the sergeant on duty and telling him that Jacques is back in Paris, hiding from creditors and police. The cowardly act of informing is not merely something she does; it embodies her personality, the most hidden recesses of her ego; it becomes Maud, the girl she had always been underneath the mask of tenderness and filial love she had worn in the beginning. Marguerite Duras makes this plain in the sentence which precedes Maud's first words to the sergeant: "And suddenly she felt as if the thing [the denunciation] became a substitute for her ego." But it does not matter how hard one tries, or what illusions one stupidly weaves around oneself. It is well-nigh impossible to create a personal, permanent identity regardless of the shape one wishes to give to it. She could neither be the understanding daughter and the affectionate sister she had pretended to be, nor could she fill the role of odious informer as an acceptable alternative; for the policeman is quick in shattering her newly acquired pose: "I don't know what you really mean . . . we looked for him, of course, The Tavarès Bank, from which your brother borrowed, was an organization of crooks. As we found his name in their files, we tried to get in touch. For a while we thought that he might be an accomplice. But actually it is he who was robbed by them. He should have complained. I don't see why you have come here. . . ."

And so there is nothing left to do but to return to Georges, to marry him "not with pleasure, rather with a certain curiosity. How would Georges appear to her now, now that she was going to belong to him forever?" As a matter of fact, their meeting at the train station of the little town of Semoic is totally devoid of warmth. She thinks more of complaining about her family than of embracing her future husband. And when he informs her, abruptly, that he remitted the 50,000 francs to the Percresses out of his own pocket, she is taken aback by his generosity, as is the reader. Her remark: "You did it to please them [her family]?" is echoed by him: "Yes . . . why not please them?" But the explanation, constituting the last line of the novel, is vague and open to a number of interpretations. Did he do it because he was really in love with Maud? Because he was taking pride in being able to act magnanimously? Or simply because, as Maud's husband, he preferred to own her free and clear?

Using a procedure that she is going to employ often in later works, Marguerite Duras leaves much to the imagination of the reader. Not only have we doubts on the couple's chance for future happiness, but we wonder too about the drowning or the murder of the girl whose body Maud had discovered; and we question what the true character of most of the novel's protagonists really is. Yet, if we do not know to what extent Maud is essentially good or basically evil; if Jacques is simply an amoral playboy or a repugnant murderer; if Georges has the qualities of a good, loving husband or would only claim his wife as he does his beloved horse and the kill of his daily hunting expeditions; if Madame Grand-Taneran is a mean, domineering woman or a victimized mother, unloved by her children whom she selflessly helps by all means at her disposal, it is because the author has been able to create complex, true-to-life characters replete with laudable and bad intentions, capable of tender and violent reactions, sometimes shrewd, sometimes calculating, but on occasion also open and sincere and able to love genuinely, for a short while, those who fill the closed circle of their subjective reality. Thus it is that we feel more sympathy than scorn for these *impudents* whom most of us resemble to a greater or lesser degree. Their efforts and their hesitations, their sporadic successes and ensuing failures are eminently recognizable by all those who have attempted, consciously, to give meaning and direction to their existence.

The unending struggle of maintaining a comfortable yet liberating relationship with the members of one's family is particularly well described by Marguerite Duras who pursues, in this novel, the general preoccupations of François Mauriac. Madame Grand-Taneran, Jacques, Maud, Henri, and even the indifferent and obscure M. Taneran try (the latter's choice of impassivity is itself an attempt, after all), awkwardly and spasmodically, to remain supremely independent in spite of the tyranny of familial bonds, that is, they try to reconcile irreconcilables, the impossible yet challenging task of all human beings. In one of those rare instances of author intrusions which betray the talented writer even in a first book, Marguerite Duras notes in Part I: "Although quite rare, there were, however, some good hours in the house of the Grand-Tanerans. Peace would come about of itself, as a sort of necessary tranquillity. Their strange enmities would have been less salient if they had not alternated with moments of respite during which they would catch their breath." It is obvious that not only the author but the characters themselves are aware (as we are in real-life, similar circumstances) that quarrels must be succeeded by peacemaking efforts in the course of which they can regroup their forces in order to renew the fight for complete self-sufficiency. Jacques, for example, "Would take pleasure in humiliating you, then he himself would reassure you so as not to lose his victim entirely." He knows, perhaps more than the others, that *l'enfer c'est les autres*,[1] for by their very existence *the others* diminish your own existence and freedom. Yet, *les autres* must be very carefully dealt with, and above all they must not be annihilated too soon; for if no ultimate understanding is possible, communication at the point of a real or imaginary knife is better than no com-

munication at all. The contradiction between our need and our
hatred of *others* is at the core of *Les Impudents,* as it is at the
core of works by many a more experienced and celebrated
novelist than Madame Duras was in 1943.[2]

This first attempt at fiction writing contains, too, a number
of brilliant stylistic sallies. They are rare, but when they occur
their quality is noticeable and announces the accomplished
author Madame Duras was going to become. In Part II, for
example, her description of Maud's first abandonment into the
arms of Durieux is a beautifully constructed passage which
shows the writer's acquaintance with the complexities of a
woman's love and a virgin's pudicity:

She guessed that he was going to approach her. Although it was only
a matter of an instant, she could not bear the imminence of his nearness. For a second, once more back to her senses, her pudicity
returned, entirely, a lucid defense mechanism that frightened her.
She closed her eyes. She had only the time to hear an interior voice
begging her to become weak; and very quickly she succumbed to that
voice and managed to liberate herself from her will, as in the wind
the leaf which snatches itself from the tree and carries itself off,
fulfilling, finally, its desire to die.

When in the same part Maud has occasion to talk with a friend,
Louise, about the many predicaments in which she finds herself, the latter, with typical feminine cruelty takes advantage
of the situation in order to show her aloofness from and her
superiority over an acquaintance in distress: "Standing, she
looked straight into Maud's eyes, as she lay at her feet; never
before would she have expressed herself with so much audacity.
She found so much pleasure in it that she was surpassing her
own intention of meanness. She listened to herself talk, and
closed her eyes, enraptured after each phrase she uttered." An
equal ability to probe deeply into the feelings of her personages,
this time in a language that is almost poetic, occurs in Part III
when Maud's own cruelty comes to the surface and she has
visions not only of Jacques in prison but of Jacques dead,

his face disfigured by fear, and on which perhaps shame would be
inscribed in little blemishes around the lips and the eyes . . . a face
feebly balanced above true sadness and which for the first time would
recall that of childhood, his childhood finally surging and being
struck by death. From that face would fly in fragments all that

intense vanity, the sempiternal possession of pleasure, the very beautiful ugliness.

And in the closing passages of the book, when Maud is prey to one of those moments of dejection that precedes her forced return to Durieux, Marguerite Duras evokes, touchingly, what might very well describe her heroine's future life next to a man she had loved but now loves much less, in the indifferent, placid, boring, provincial atmosphere of his home: "She did not think of anyone, of anything except of the horrific abyss of the day in which she was slowly being plunged, and which seemed to close upon herself as an ocean on a sinking ship that was still alive, too slow in dying, too slow in reaching the bottom."

But in spite of these and other similarly remarkable parts, *Les Impudents* remains a modest first step in the career of Marguerite Duras. While readers can easily recognize the contradictions in the character of her personages and the struggles in which they are engaged, there is only little catharsis to be derived from an essentially domestic drama which lacks the limitless consequences of those described by writers having analogous concerns (François Mauriac, Georges Bernanos, Julien Green, and many another Roman Catholic author). With the exception of Maud, no other member of the Taneran family is tortured by remorse or by a consciousness of sin or even wrongdoing. Their conflicts appear pale in comparison to the simultaneous attraction of religion and voluptuousness we find in the characters of Mauriac, for example. Unlike the Catholic writer who is prompted by his faith to see in many daily occurrences the possible spiritual repercussions of otherwise insignificant events (and thereby enhance the tense, evocative power and the dimensions of his story), Marguerite Duras, an apparently areligious novelist, does not manage to discover any patterns in the chaos of daily existence, nor to stir the reader's imagination by relating calamitous episodes in the life of her *impudents.* The probable murder of one of Jacques's girl friends looms in the background, of course, but it takes place only after we have read almost half the book; and at any rate, this violent outer conflict, if it did occur, is not sufficient to break the monotony of the inner one, either in Jacques or in Maud.

This inner landscape pervades the novel and, engaging as it

is at times, the slow rhythm with which it moves limits the
scope of the writer who seems to lack range, movement, and
variety. Her means, compactness, economy, poetry, reveal indeed
the hidden physical and spiritual aspirations of characters whose
lusts and frustrations lurk in their deepest fibers, to surge out,
occasionally, and break through to the surface in perceptible
events. But these are not presented in careful completeness,
and the personages remain, for the most part, stripped of the
wealth of activities that usually go into the making of a
human life.

Acting as an even more irritating determent to the quality
of the book are the all-too-frequent author's comments on the
heroes and heroines she creates. In this context, the criticism
that Jean-Paul Sartre and others have leveled at Mauriac[3] can
be raised against Marguerite Duras' tendency, in *Les Impudents*,
to appear often on the scene of her novel and to direct sur-
reptitiously the point of view of characters whose acts likewise
she openly guides. But Madame Duras is not a Catholic writer,
afraid that the novelist in her might betray her religion; and
the Tanerans and the Pecresses should have been given more
freedom than they were awarded. As it is, the less ordered,
less tense, less esthetically satisfying fiction of *Les Impudents*
cannot sustain lasting reader's interest or literary validity.

II La Vie tranquille

Like *Les Impudents,* Marguerite Duras' second novel remained
unnoticed at the time of its publication in 1944. The furious
battles of the last months of World War II did not favor large
sales of a book that related still another domestic drama. Some
recent criticism, however, has deemed it necessary to go back
at least to *La Vie tranquille* in order to locate the beginning
of the writer's talent at work. The reputable Bernard Pingaud,
for example, precedes his analysis of Marguerite Duras with
the following candid invitation: "Let us reread this astonishing
book of which no one ever speaks, *La Vie tranquille*."[4] And his
discussion of the novel concludes with some of the most complimentary remarks to be found in *Ecrivains d'aujour'hui 1940-
1960*: "It was necessary, we think, to insist on *La Vie tranquille*.
It is a masterpiece and an unknown masterpiece, if not an
ignored one. The second novel of Marguerite Duras in chrono-

logical order explains and announces the rest of her output as a first panel of a great structure."[5]

La Vie tranquille is a touching story written in the first person and told with a great sobriety of means. Because of frequent understatements which help to emphasize the platitudes of life, it is rich in the never-ending search, conscious or unconscious, ardent or passive, for an elusive absolute, a role, a pose, a mask—a reason.

Francou, a twenty-five-year-old girl, inscribes in her notebook the behavior of friends and relatives in her provincial town, also her feelings, her fears, her nothingness which strives to exist. But Francou is not alone. The mediocrity of life weighs on the others with the same intensity, causing human beings to vegetate, the living to become dead or dormant, the inanimate to become overpowering and crushing.[6] Nothing ever happens. Francou's mother is "neither happy nor unhappy." She gives the impression that "she is not with us, that she is with passing time, traveling with it. . . ." The shepherd, Clément, "prefers nothing to no one, no one to nothing. He is careful about having any opinion, they say he is old, they say he is dumb, he does not do anyone any harm, nor any good. . . ." Later, Francou comments: "I do not think he is leading a human life; his thoughts begin with daylight and end at dusk." About herself she admits: "I was a nobody, I had no name, no face . . . I was nothing. My steps made no noise, no one heard me, I was disturbing no one." Elsewhere, she adds: "I thought of my age, I thought of all those who were asleep in this house, and I heard time eat away at us like an army of rats." When Tiène, a friend of Nicolas, her brother, visits the family in order to make the acquaintance of Francou, the girl remarks: "I warned him that it would be a silly idea; here, it would be as if no one is ever around."

Like the heroes of the New Novel of the late 1950s and early 1960s, the personages of this story have become dehumanized (if they had ever been human), that is to say divested of incarnation. They are deprived of that time which can be divided into past, present, and future. They are like time, passing, intemporal. They are shapeless, absent, unaware of the possibility of choosing, of becoming reincarnated. Life for them is so meaningless and static that inactivity becomes, if not an ideal worthy of pursuit like that of the contemplative Buddhists, a means of hibernation void of happiness, but also of desire. That is not to say that these personages do not experience rare and excessive feelings, or that they are not capable of committing monstrous acts. Nicolas, for example, kills his uncle, Jérôme. The murder is a trivial, senseless action, but it will awaken the others, it will force them to choose. Not all, however, for the parents and the shepherd are already too old and too intemporal; and, although they keep on breathing, their apparent existence is only a tropism, an uncontrolled response to uncomprehended stimuli.[7] But the rest of the family is immediately prompted to act. Clémence, Nicolas' wife and mistress of the murdered uncle, flees. She is replaced by Luce, who had always been in love with Nicolas, but who could not interlope so long as the wife was still present. She represents the intrusion in a de-humanized household of a passionate, exuberant, and humane influence. Her entrance marks the end of a tranquil life of indifference and absence. It is the beginning of the individual-ization of the others. When Luce seems to forget her first love and becomes enamoured of Tiène, Nicolas commits suicide and Francou is obliged to take a stand, to con Tiène into marrying her, into becoming "a being of fortune and misfortune, one who must choose her among all girls, one who must choose, among all empires, that which is lost in advance, that which can never be found, the empire called happiness."

Tranquil life, then, is nothing but a way of non-existing. One can grow old that way and die without having lived, without having experienced suffering or joy, dragged by and with time, absurdly, unaware of even the closest calamities. But the younger ones have a chance at incarnation, at life, sometimes derisively (murder, suicide), sometimes in a reasonable fashion (falling in love, marrying). But no matter, for in either case incarnation is utopian: suicide is a negative solution and involves only a momentary acceptance of life because of the appeal of its opposite, death; and love and marriage without the hope of happiness constitute a mere adoption of common practices which, in time, will only result in a return of the process of dehuman-ization ephemerally interrupted. For the mediocrity of life is a redoubtable foe: one can avoid the battle and die slowly, as did Francou's parents; or seek solution through murder and suicide, as in the case of Nicolas; or, like Francou, give onself the illusion of passionate feelings while still possessing that lucidity which makes one aware of the futility of it all.

Armand Hoog, with the exception of Bernard Pingaud the only critic who seemed to have paid more than a cursory attention to *La Vie tranquille,* noted unspecified similarities between the American novel and Marguerite Duras' second attempt at fiction: "We must render unto Caesar what is Caesar's and to Uncle Sam as novelist his due. The French have been only too tempted to imitate America. We have all too often been presented with sham Steinbeck and pseudo-Caldwell. In the years following the Liberation, the evil was at its height. . . . Marguerite Duras began, then, by drawing in some measure her inspiration from the American novel. That is apparent in *La Vie tranquille* (1944), a pleasant but somewhat disconcerting narrative, a curious mixture of the farmyard and Saint-Germain-des-Prés, of urban nausea and rustic odors, of Erskine Caldwell and Jean-Paul Sartre."[8] Caldwell, famous here and on the Continent for his *Tobacco Road* (1932) and *God's Little Acre* (1933), may have influenced indeed the general tone of *La Vie tranquille.* The American author's sympathy for the underdogs of whom he wrote is matched by the French writer whose pen is also, often, in this novel (and in others), as unabashedly obscene as that of Caldwell. Like him, Marguerite Duras feels for her heroes and heroines. One recalls that she became familiar with the extreme poverty in and around Saigon in her youth, and that she must have known the dullness of life of the *montagnards* whose terrestrial passage is usually devoid of even the possibility of joy. But the appeal of Caldwell (and surely William Faulkner also) is superimposed on her Far Eastern experience. Their descriptions of the decadent South, of its ruined farms and poor whites clinging obstinately to an uncertain past, provided her with images that few French writers of her generation managed to ignore. Yet, if the punch of Caldwell's vocabulary is there, the obscene passages are not destined to *épater le bourgeois* (an accusation often made against the American novelist who, on account of it, had to defend himself in court on numerous occasions), they are not there for their own sake. Francou's sensitivity erases any possible charge of undue awareness of the intimate parts of her body: "How hypocritical I am! Nothing can be seen of that pit which is there, between my legs. The one to discover it will believe that

it has just opened under him, through his efforts. It is per-
fidiousness and innocence. . . . Or the bottom of that pit is at
the same time a shelter, the only shelter before Heaven and
one of the last walls to be left in the world. I can't do anything
about it. I am nothing next to it." Her concern for sex appears
eminently feminine, a touching blend of "I am a one man's
woman" idea, as she says at one point, and an early nostalgia
for the limitations that fidelity imposes:

When men pass in front of me on the beach, half naked, I think of
the body of Tiène . . . Tiène is the man I love. He will be the only
one, perhaps, to whom I shall be able to offer that cavity of freshness.
Yet, he exists among all the others whom I shall never know,[9] yet
there are the others. They exist. With their smiles. I shall not see them
seek me. I shall not watch them discover me. I shall not listen to them
fall on me, with utmost confidence, and get up confusedly, like those
birds that rise from the beach where the wind has thrown them.

The question, How can a peasant girl like Francou analyze
profoundly the most hidden meannig of her complex feelings?
imposes itself. And unless we are content with the possibility
that she is more intelligent and more sensitive than most in
the class to which she belongs and in the farm surroundings in
which she lives, we must assume, as in the previous novel,
that Marguerite Duras lends her own acute mental receptiveness
to the characters of her imagination whose actions and reactions
she guides. While the validity of such a procedure is often
tenable, it seems that credibility suffers to a degree when the
sagacity of the writer is bestowed upon a personage like Francou,
one who lacks the background required for the acquisition and
development of a superior intelligence. This is perhaps what
Armand Hoog had in mind when he referred to the "curious
mixture," in *La Vie tranquille*, of "urban nausea and rustic
odors." Actually, the theme of nausea, a few years old among
the literary elite of 1944,[10] is quite distinct in a number of
characters in the novel, but especially in the heroine. *De trop*
at first, just as Roquentin was before he discovered the pleasures
of the world of music when he heard the jazz recording of
Some of These Days, Francou assumes an identity and becomes
reincarnated (although Roqentin did not since *La Nausée* ends
without any apparent solution)[11] when she realizes that she
has fallen in love:

Then [when she thinks of Tiène] I believe that I am a woman. That I am alive as a woman, not as just anything, as a woman only. I shall not dare say that up to now I did not hope to be also alive as a being belonging to a different species. To run one day up the hill like the dog of Clément. To spread one day my branches like the magnolia in the backyard. I did not confess to myself that it seemed impossible to be a disguised dog, a disguised tree. Now I am aware of it [that she cannot be anything but a woman] and I know that it cannot be otherwise.

But the temporariness of Francou's incarnation (from nothingness to womanhood) does not deceive anyone, least of all Francou. Much like Maud, the heroine of *Les Impudents*, Francou anticipates, toward the end of the novel, what the future holds for her. That mediocrity of which she and others had been so painfully aware all along will eventually set in, and, she says, there will not be anything else to do but to count "the years which are left for me to live . . . ten, twenty, forty years. Nothing will mark them, nothing can happen to me." She will then become like her mother and father: she will await death placidly, living without desires, without passion that tranquil life that inters, sooner or later, all who accept it and all who fight it. She concludes:

I shall watch the land become covered with snow at times, at times with fruits, at times with mud, at times with the white of engagement parties, with milk, with catastrophies, with tears. . . . One day I shall no longer love Tiène. On second thought, do I love him still? One day I shall live without the memory of Tiène, a whole day without his name wetting my lips even once. One day I shall die.

The sadness that emanates from *La Vie tranquille* touches the reader much more effectively than the moderate pathos in *Les Impudents*. Passages such as the one just quoted make identification with Francou's unsolvable problems so easy that we cannot avoid feeling disturbed about the uncertainty of our own sentiments and about the lack of durability of everything that marks our existence. Similar apprehensions that we may have nourished all along come to the surface now. They cease to be carefully guarded secrets and, after we have read the novel, we begin to realize that they are not so personal or so rare as we might have imagined. And so it is that we feel only a qualified loneliness now. We discover that we are all crushed by the mediocrity of life, that we all fluctuate, to our death, between years of boredom, depression, and spiritual hunger, and fleeting hours during which happiness seems possible, for a while, for a very short while, for the briefest but most rewarding moment. There is a suspicion of catharsis in this realization: for if *la vie tranquille* crushes the whole of humanity, it crushes the individual less; and a hint, too, of the worthiness of life: for like Francou, who at the very end looks forward to sleeping in Tiène's arms (in the arms of a man whom she might still or might no longer love, but whom she will certainly stop loving one day), we too ought to be prompted, the author implies, to seize upon every remote instant of joy. In a *vie tranquille* each moment of an even approximate state of well-being is a momentous moment. The clarity of Marguerite Duras' message is especially obvious today to the post-*Myth of Sisyphus* generation.[12] Little wonder that, while it could not attain wide popularity in the war-torn period of the novel's publication, *La Vie tranquille* captures the attention of more recent critics who see in it a brilliant invitation to *un-tranquil* life extended by an unknown author who, surprisingly, only once before had tried her hand at the writing of fiction.

III   Un Barrage contre le Pacifique

"Fed up?" asked Suzanne.

He raised his eyes, saw her sitting there on the edge of his bed in her torn dress.

"It's nothing. Did she hurt you?"

"That's not it . . ."

"You fed up, too?"

"Oh, I don't know."

"What's bothering you?"

"Everything," said Suzanne. "I'm like you, I don't know."

"Hell," said Joseph, "we've got to think about her, too. She's old, we can't imagine, and she's more fed up than we are. And for her, it's finished . . ."

"What's finished?"

"Fun. Good times. She never had much fun and she'll never have any now, she's too old for it now, there's not much time left to her . . . Go, go to bed. I want to lie down."

Suzanne stood up. As she went out, Joseph asked her:

"Did you sleep with him or didn't you?"

"No, I didn't sleep with him."

"I believe you. It's not just the business of you going to bed with a man. But he's not the one to go to bed with, he's a swine. And tomorrow you've got to tell him not ever to come here again."

"Never again?"

"Never again."

"So then, what will happen?"

"I don't know," said Joseph. "We'll see."

This piece of dialogue, whose tone is duplicated throughout *Un Barrage contre le Pacifique*,[13] reveals the growing influence of the American-type novel on Marguerite Duras. "*Un Barrage contre le Pacifique*," Germaine Brée stated, was a story in the manner of the American novel, à la Hemingway."[14] She does not go any further than this, but the passage cited seems to conform to the following general comments of Maurice Blanchot on Madame Duras' books:

Dialogue, under the influence of several American writers, has assumed an expressive insignificance: more worn out than in reality, a little above the empty word which suffices in daily life; when someone speaks, it is his refusal to speak which then becomes apparent; his speech is his silence: obscure, violent, saying nothing beyond itself, it has an abrupt weight, a will to emit words rather than to speak. Or simply, as is the case with Hemingway, an exquisite manner to express itself a little above zero, which is a shrewd way to make us believe in some sort of intense life, emotion or thought, a classic and honest way which is often successful and to which the melancholic talent of Hemingway lends a wealth of variations.[15]

But the characters of *Un Barrage contre le Pacifique* speak often, and they often have something to say over and above the immediate meaning of the words used. Their speeches are not always clear. However (they will become foreboding and cryptic in the anti-novels), they draw from and contribute to the violence of the atmosphere, and they do indeed suggest, as with Hemingway, an overpowering intensity of feeling and intellectual activity.

Madame Duras' third novel takes place in her native country, Indochina. At the end of the nineteenth century, somewhere in northern France a gullible schoolmistress saw a poster inviting French men and women to an exotic life abroad. "Young people," the poster assured, "a fortune awaits you in the Colonies." Ma and her husband, also a teacher, fell prey to the advertisement and sailed, in 1899, for the promising faraway land. This is part

of the background to which the author refers in the course of
the novel, for the story begins in the 1920s, long after the husband's death, when the family passes through a period of financial and moral decay. Life had been modestly pleasant in the
beginning, even prosperous. They had both taught in State
Schools; then, when Joseph and Suzanne were born, Ma gave
French lessons to the natives, and her husband was appointed
headmaster of a private institution.

After his death, however, there was never enough money. In
addition to language lessons Ma was forced to engage in piano
instruction and even to hire herself as pianist at the Eden Cinema
where she worked, under the most miserable conditions, for some
ten years. Economizing continuously, she was able to bring up
her children and to put enough money aside to buy from the
cadastral government of the Colony a concession of land. She,
her children, and an old servant worked the land assiduously,
hoping for a harvest that would enable her to pay off the mortgage and retain the land which could be taken away from her,
after the lapse of a certain period, if it had not been properly
cultivated. But the floods came, and everything was ruined.
Unflinching in her hopes and courageous enough to fight the
blind onslaught of Nature, Ma persuaded the natives in the
surrounding area to build, together with her and for the common
good, a barrier, a sea wall that would protect the crops. The
crabs promptly ate it away, and the next year the dyke col-
lapsed. The year after was a repetition of the year before until,
after several attempts, she had to give up any aspiration at making
a go of her harvest and mortgage plans. Ma took to pills, then,
and to extensive periods of drowsiness and sleep; Joseph, twenty,
took to women, an old beat-up Citroen B12 that he would often
take apart and put together again, and long sessions of listening
to scratched records playing ceaselessly on a rotten phonograph;
Suzanne, seventeen, was content to wait patiently on the road
from Ram to Kam. It was the only road, "so you couldn't miss
the way. All the same, the future might hold something, and
Suzanne kept on hoping. Maybe one day a man would stop
because he had seen her sitting near the bridge. Why not? Pos-
sibly he would like her looks and would offer to take her to the
city."

Into this sick atmosphere of starving natives and degenerating
whites living side by side but in the most segregated fashion

(Madame Duras, as American authors deriding the South often do, mocks the habits of the whites: "The whites . . . were very clean. As soon as they arrived they would learn to wash every day, as little children are made to. They would also learn to wear the Colonial uniform, suits of spotless white, the color of immunity and innocence"), a very ugly and very rich Britisher stumbles, a Mr. Jo, who promptly falls in love with Suzanne and proceeds to make her a number of gifts: a new phonograph, which she gives to her brother, an expensive diamond, the sale of which she also entrusts to Joseph. In exchange for these and other presents he would like to sleep with her. Suzanne would, and her mother and brother would not object (actually they teach her, at times subtly, at times openly, how to get the most out of Mr. Jo), were it not for the fact that his physical appearance is equally repugnant to all. And so a compromise is reached: she will simply show herself to him, naked, while in the process of taking a shower. But the arrangement does not last: Ma would like Mr. Jo to marry Suzanne, he would like some more tangible proof of her affection for him; and at any rate, his father would never agree. Mr. Jo disappears, Joseph sells the diamond for 20,000 francs, Ma uses the money to pay a minute part of her debts, and the family soon finds itself in the same financial and moral crisis it had been in at the beginning.

The jungle type of existence against which the natives and the whites living in the plains of Indochina must struggle is duplicated, in *Un Barrage contre le Pacifique,* by the inner, undomesticated life of the personages. Joseph, who hunts frequently, sometime even at night, seeks to liberate himself from the prison of poverty and from the hermetically closed cell of false hopes that his mother entertains. The kill of his hunting expeditions puts meat on the family's table; his pursuit of women nets him a rich, generous, not so young but still pretty catch who supports him financially and sexually, and in whose company he will eventually leave his home forever. His sister, equally caught in the circle of indigence common to all, and in the messy web of Ma's *barrages* (against the sea, against the cadastral government, against Mr. Jo, indeed against the universe), tries to attain freedom through a clever compromise between virginity and prostitution; and after Mr. Jo disappears, through the gratuitous act of giving herself to Agosti, a local white whom she does not love and whose sentiments for her are, at best, uncertain; finally,

by breaking entirely with the past in refusing to marry Agosti
and in accompanying Joseph in his flight to an unknown destination.

But before the final steps can be taken, before the cutting of
the umbilical cord, it is necessary for Ma to die. This she oblig-
ingly, finally does, and in spite of the son's and daughter's pro-
testations to the contrary, in spite of their tears, it is apparent
that only now they have been born, that only now they can
really breathe, unchecked, fully, with their own thoracic spasms
and for their unique benefit. Suzanne and Joseph have now their
own measure of validity; they have broken out of the tight
quarters of a paranoiac's inner jungle; they have assumed their
own, their very personal role. Of course, this role remains vague.
Perhaps it is no more than a pose that will fade away, a delusion.
For where are they going and what will they become? Or, to be
more precise, how more deeply will they sink into the questionable world of prostitutes and gigolos? No matter, for now they
no longer feel as they did in the dialogue quoted above; they
are no longer fed up, lethargic; and if delusion there is, the
delusion is theirs and it is all the more real because it is so very
fragile and so very temporary.

The initial reception of American reviewers was mildly enthusiastic: "For U.S. readers, Author Duras' characters will have
something of the fascination and strangeness of people from an
exotic, outdoor *Snake Pit*. In France . . . it should confirm the
widespread French conviction that there's no place like home,"
stated the anonymous critic of *Times*.[16] In England, critical
acclaim limited itself to mention of the similarity between the
locale of the book and the American Southen states. The following is an example of the rather cool appreciation *Un Barrage
contre le Pacifique* was accorded after its translation under the
title *A Sea of Troubles*: "[the book] is not any more cheerful than
one would expect from the title. It is about poor whites on a
decaying small-holding, not, this time, in the Southern states, but
in French Indochina, or the territory which used to be known by
that name . . . it makes splendid reading for anyone who is in
the mood to read about tropical hardships and demoralizations."[17]

Reviewers became more enthusiastic, however, after other
novels by the author began appearing. They were inclined to
check Duras' earlier works and they began to discover qualities
that had gone unnoticed in the past. Gérard d'Houville, for

example, preceded his remarks on *Le Marin de Gibraltar* with a
laudatory appreciation of *Un Barrage*. He declared: [the book]
revealed to me her talent, so original, so daring, so new. I have
much admired that novel."[18] D'Houville obviously meant that
fiction à la Hemingway was an audacious and novel approach
for French letters at the time of Madame Duras' publication.
The distinguished Gaëtan Picon also stated his admiration for
the book, in particular "the complexity and the electicism of
means in *Un Barrage contre le Pacifique*".[19] Armand Hoog, who
likewise had spoken of the relationship between American novelists and Marguerite Duras, had the following to say about the
work:[20] "I discover upon rereading it the impression I had in
opening the volume nearly ten years ago: my appreciation and a
certain disappointment. Such a vigorous writer who draws so
heavily upon foreign models."[21] But the criticism is immediately
qualified: "It is well perhaps to insist somewhat on that *Barrage*
which placed Madame Duras in the front ranks of young French
novelists."[22] Writing much later than d'Houville, Jacques Guicharnaud, concerned more with the subsequent anti-fiction of the
author, mentions *Un Barrage contre le Pacifique* for the virility of
its characters, for their courage. He adds that it (as the later
Le Marin de Gibraltar) were "early novels . . . in which Marguerite Duras was still somewhat influenced by a conventional
novel form [conventional at the time, as the American-type novel
was]."[23] Yet, taking a second look, he does not fail to perceive
that "the endless repetitions in the seemingly pointless and interminable conversations [the dialogue quoted above, for example]
finish by producing an effect of strangeness, the feeling of an
exasperating and monotonous waste of time, which appears to
be the very substance of the characters' lives."[24] In the very
American-type dialogue, then, Guicharnaud sees the seeds of
the New Novel, a form which the author will embrace more and
more as her pen becomes increasingly mature and experienced.

As a matter of fact, *Un Barrage contre le Pacifique* contains a
number of themes and stylistic procedures to be espoused later
by many anti-novelists, Marguerite Duras included. The characters' reliance on things (the Citroen B12, the phonograph, the
diamond) to prove their participation in life, for example; also
their common dependence on an animal at the very beginning
of the book, in order to prove their participation in life as intellectual beings and in order to avoid loneliness: "All three of

them had thought it was a good idea to buy that horse . . . To begin with, it was an idea — which showed that they were still capable of having ideas. Then, owning a horse made them feel less lonely, for it linked them to the outside world. Thanks to the horse, they could still manage to get something out of that world . . . and they could bring it back to their isolated piece of salt-soaked plain, to the three of them soaked in boredom and bitterness."

Solitude and boredom are ills constantly decried by the followers of the New School, and Marguerite Duras does not fail to share in similar apprehensions. The horse dies, of course, almost as soon as it is purchased. And whatever other escapes the personages think of, vanish sooner or later: the diamond has to be sold; the money received for it disappears into the pockets of creditors; need of further funds makes the sale of the phonograph imperative also; Mr. Jo himself becomes part of the general evanescence.[25] In the case of Suzanne, company is so painfully absent that she has no recourse but to sit by the side of the road, waiting: "But no car stopped in front of the bungalow. Sometimes Suzanne wistfully recalled Monsieur Jo's car and the time when it had been stationed every day in front of the bungalow. At least it was a car that stopped. Even an empty car would have been better than no car at all. Now it was as though the bungalow were invisible, as though she herself, near the bridge, were invisible." The wait is futile, just as the purchase of the horse had been. Solitude and boredom cannot be eliminated. There are no cars, there are no drivers; and the possibility of invisibleness of the bungalow and of herself casts doubt on the existence of things and beings.

Frequently, too, Madame Duras employs clichés, banalities, repetitiveness, and circular explanations that fail purposely to explain: "Ma, alone at her table, did not stop yawning. She was very tired, because she had had many misfortunes and she was old and not used to laughing. It was that laughing that had worn her out."

However, what distinguishes *Un Barrage contre le Pacifique* from a real anti-novel is not only the clarity of the plot and the ability of the reviewer to summarize it, but also a constant undertone of hope in most of its characters in spite of the repeated setbacks they suffer: Ma's trust in dykes, for instance; Suzanne's hope in meeting a man she might fall in love with; Joseph's confidence in the desirability of a suspect but new way of life. Such expectations, already alluded to above,[26] will constitute the main difference between the author's later publications and those of contemporary writers whose allegiance to the New School is closer than that of Marguerite Duras.

Yet, *Un Barrage contre le Pacifique* did not draw only upon foreign models, nor was it simply an American-type novel which contained various anti-novel characteristics. The author drew also from her own, previously published books, as well as from the vast traditions of French literature.

It is interesting to note, for example, that in her first three novels a brother has a major role to play. In *Les Impudents,* Jacques had had a great deal to do with Maud's evolvement from an apparently tender, affectionate human being into a hateful, avenging, and inimical woman; conversely, in *La Vie tranquille,* Nicolas' murder of his uncle forced Francou to choose and facilitated his sister's reincarnation into a woman in love, ready and willing to assume the social bond of marriage and at least to go through the motions of a normal life; in *Un Barrage contre le Pacifique* Joseph plays both a destructive and a salutary role in the existence of Suzanne: on the one hand his roguishness, his violence, and his lack of scruples teach his sister how to take advantage of others (her mother is not nearly so effective a teacher as Joseph because the former's instructions remain on a verbal level only, while the latter's recommendations are always corroborated by vivid examples) and how to be dishonest while maintaining an appearance of virtue; on the other hand, it is he who provides her with the means for escape[27] and with a certain amount of hope by allowing her to accompany him and his mistress. To be sure, whatever changes each brother manages to effect in his respective sister are temporary changes and rather questionable in terms of standard morality. At present, however, suffice it to point to the fact that the theme of a redoubtably strong brother-sister relationship is a constant in the first three novels of Marguerite Duras.

Equally apparent is the author's acquaintance with and recollection of the theme of the influence of one's readings on one's life. Since the Romantic period this is a standard topic in French literature. Those familiar with Gustave Flaubert's *Madame Bovary* (1857), for example, remember the impact on Emma of the fanciful books she had read in her days at the convent.

Likewise, Marguerite Duras shows the influence of Romantic
literature on Suzanne. Her heroine did not have the education
of Emma, but she did read one book and she did see a number
of motion pictures:

In the only novel she had read, as in the films that she had seen
since, the words *I love you* were pronounced but once, in the course
of a conversation between lovers which lasted barely a few minutes but
which concluded months of waiting or ended a terrible separation,
infinite griefs. Never yet had Suzanne heard the words addressed to
her. For a long time she had believed that it was infinitely more
serious to say them than to surrender to a man after having said them.
She had believed that the words could be said but once in her whole
life and that afterwards never, her whole life-long, could they be said
again, under pain of bringing upon herself an abominable dishonor.
Now she knew that she had been mistaken. You could say the words
spontaneously, in an outburst of desire, and you could say them even
to prostitutes.

Like Emma, then, and like countless other Romantics, Suzanne
begins by learning about love from fictional characters (in a
book, in movies). She concludes, as Emma did, that there is
something absolute and eternal about love, for it can only come
about after obstacles are conquered, after suffering and tears.
In this sense, her early views are not unlike those expounded in
La Carte de Tendre.[28] But life has a different lesson to teach her,
and the reality she discovers (that one can say the words *I love
you* more than once, and that one can say them at the morally
wrong time and to morally unworthy persons) is a painful reality,
one that is difficult to accept and in which it is difficult to participate. When she gives herself to Agosti, for example, and when
she realizes that she is naked in front of him, she imagines that
it is for the first time that a man observes her that way: "She
had forgotten that Monsieur Jo had seen her like that, for the
phonograph and the diamond." And because she is not really in
love, because her first act of lovemaking did not conclude "months
of waiting or ended a terrible separation," she refuses to take part
in it as she might have otherwise. Instead, she simply allows
herself to be "in his hands, adrift with the world [and to] let him
do as he would, as it had to be."
Many other passages in *Un Barrage contre le Pacifique* seem
to draw heavily upon other domestic sources, notably the revolutionary, leftist preachings of Emile Zola in such novels as

Germinal (1885) or *La Terre* (1887). These passages reveal an anti-colonial attitude on the part of Madame Duras a few years before the French society was ready to accept such an attitude. The author's firsthand knowledge of the abuses of cadastral authorities in Indochina led her to generalize and to condemn all colonial arrangements. To prove the uprightness of her position, she devoted many pages in the present novel to pointing to a number of specific evils that nourished her anger and her revolt. These pages betray a style that is reminiscent of the polemics of fighters for social justice in general, of Zola in particular, as the following verb-studded sentence shows: "On the fifteen land concessions of the plain of Kam, they had settled, ruined, driven off, resettled and again ruined and driven off perhaps a hundred families." Madame Duras' wrath is at its height when she describes the plight of starving, sick, and dying native children. She points to their lack of food, of love, of companionship. They roamed the gutters in groups, followed by dogs only, for their excrements provided the canines with their sole source of nourishment. They were born, suffered a little while, then died. There was no variation to the pattern:

There were children as there were rains, fruits, floods. They came each year, by periodical tides, or, if you like, by crops of burgeonings. Every woman of the plain, as long as she was young enough to be desired by her husband, had her child each year. . . . This went on regularly, with the rhythm of plant-life, as if, in a deep, long inhalation, each year, the body of each woman took in and swelled with child, expelled in an exhalation a child and then, in a second inhalation, took in another. [And] they died in such numbers that they were no longer mourned, and for many long years it had been the custom to bury them without ceremony. . . . The children returned simply to the earth like wild mangoes falling from high branches. . . . Some of the children drowned. Others, still, died of sunstroke or became blinded with the sun. Others filled themselves with the same worms that devoured the stray dogs and died, suffocated.

The narrative becomes even more shocking when the writer decides to use the device of sarcasm:

And it was very needful that they die, some of them. The plain was narrow and the sea would not recede. . . . It was very needful that some of them die. For if, during a few years only, the children of the plain had ceased to die, the plain would have been overrun with them to such an extent that, no doubt, for lack of the means to nourish them, it would have been necessary to give them to the dogs or perhaps to expose them at the edge of the forest.

And at the end of the book, when Joseph gets ready to leave, he makes a speech to those who are left behind, urging them to rise against the oppressive authorities:

I'm leaving everything to you, especially the guns. . . . See to it that whatever you do you make a good job of it. You must take their corpses into the forest . . . in two days' time there won't be anything left of them. Burn their clothes in the brush fires you light at night. Be careful about their shoes and their buttons. Bury the ashes of the fires afterwards. Pitch their car far off in the *rac*. Use the buffaloes, they will drag it to the bank, you will put big stones on the seats . . . it will be sunk out of sight and nothing will remain. Above all, don't get caught. And see to it that you don't any of you confess. Or else, let all of you confess. Together. If you are a thousand people that have done something together, no one can do anything against you.

It is obvious that Joseph speaks for Madame Duras, especially in view of the author's previous intrusions into the story.

As a matter of fact, such intrusions, as I have pointed out in analyzing *Les Impudents* and *La Vie tranquille,* often detract from the central plot and distract the reader: chapter 12 in Part II of the novel, in which Joseph narrates to Suzanne the circumstances surrounding his chance meeting with Lina, the woman whose gigolo he was going to become, drags on and on, and it is all the more monotonous since it is a flashback and the reader does not get a feeling of direct participation; equally boring is chapter 14 of Part II, which contains an eleven-page letter from Ma to the cadastral agent at Kam.

One other shortcoming is worth mentioning, that is the excesses of the author's brutal realism in the language used and sometime in the situations described. While such language contributes often to the over-all impact of the story, it is doubtful that sentences like: "At times, when she [Ma] had been taking too many pills, she would wet in her bed," add much to the general decaying and dehumanizing picture the writer had already drawn. Likewise, pre- and post-intercourse narratives appear to be too long, overtly shocking and at least on one occasion bordering on the scandalous.[29] Mention has already been made of the length excesses in chapter 12, Part II; moreover, Joseph's account of his conquest of Lina is replete with physical details that leave little to the imagination. Also, chapter 21 of Part II, relating the lovemaking scene between Suzanne and Agosti, contains the following passage of dubious worth: "what had counted had been his gestures with her, the attitude of his body towards hers . . . He had taken out his handkerchief and had wiped off the blood that had run down her thighs. Then, before leaving, he had put a corner of the bloody handkerchief in his mouth, without disgust, and with his saliva he had cleaned away once more the dried blood stains." The conclusion that the author draws for her heroine does not necessarily follow and is vague both in the French and in the English text: "That love could abolish physical differences to such an extent she would never forget."[30] It can be argued, I suppose, that Agosti's gestures have little to do with love and much more to do with lovemaking. Actually, the act of *drinking* the possessed girl's virginity is an unusual extension of Agosti's great desire for her. It can be interpreted, however, as a self-debasing display of his belief in a personal unworthiness to possess such a beautiful girl as Suzanne.

The heroine appears to reach this conclusion and to be touched. But it is not in the robust, self-assured, girl-chaser character that Agosti has to consider himself inferior to or undeserving of any girl's favor. Moreover, Suzanne's ability to experience such a subtle feeling as the one the author attributes to her, and never to forget it, would signal a sensitivity in the personage for which we have not been adequately prepared. For after all, a similar sensitivity is not in keeping with her previous compromise between virginity and prostitution; nor does it conform with her constant abuse of Mr. Jo, her interest in material possessions, her shrewdness, her unqualified admiration of Joseph and, more particularly, of all that is morally objectionable in him. What Marguerite Duras is asking the reader to believe is that, when reincarnation occurs, unpredictability is no longer a valid argument. Perhaps this is so for a while. Perhaps, for a moment, Suzanne is capable of performing acts and of feeling emotions that neither she nor we could have anticipated. But in the end she does abandon Agosti and she does flee with her brother: she was not, therefore, permanently touched by her lover's *love* for her. And so it appears that Marguerite Duras, as she has done in the past and will occasionally do in the future, intervenes in order to bestow upon her characters a glow, an aura that they do not necessarily possess.

But *Un Barrage contre le Pacifique* remains a powerful novel, a tense account of life in a colonial society that is at the antipode of that pictured in advertising posters. Sea walls are eaten away by crabs, children are devoured by worms or die of starvation, familiar bonds are pecked at by monetary problems, and human degradation reigns supreme. Yet, Ma's hope, until almost the very end, rises against the multifarious calamities that besiege her family, her people. It is this hope that we tend to recall, rather than the final moments of drugged drowsiness, decomposition, and death. For while barriers collapse, as inimical Nature reclaims its dominance over living matter, other walls will be built; and while builders die, others will take their place. Not Suzanne, not Joseph, who give up the struggle; but perhaps the peasants who are left behind and to whom Joseph entrusts his guns. Surely this struggle will not be an easy one, and chances are very good that it will abort. As a matter of fact, subsequent events in Indochina have only compounded the misery of its inhabitants. But minor and temporary sources of consolation exist, and it is even possible, sometime, to arrive at definitions of human satisfaction in the face of the most insuperable odds. In one of the saddest, most tenderly evocative passages of the book Marguerite Duras comments: "to go every evening to the movies represented, along with motoring, one of the forms which human happiness could take. In sum, everything that carried you off, everything that bore you up — whether your soul or your body, whether along the road or along the truer-than-life dream-paths of the silver screen, everything that could give the hope of living quickly the slow experience of adolescence — these things represented happiness."

IV Le Marin de Gibraltar

The nameless hero and his mistress, Anna, mention Hemingway four times in Marguerite Duras' fourth novel. Much of the story takes place on a boat on the high seas, and there is even an expedition in the interior of Africa to the Kilimanjaro Mountains. Repeatedly, the anonymous hero speaks of his desire to write an *American* novel on his adventures and those of his friends. At one point, pressed on this question by his mistress: "Why American?" he replies: "Because of the whiskey."

Actually, whiskey is consumed in great quantities by the protagonists of *Le Marin de Gibraltar,* from about the middle of the book until its end: "I drank whiskey to restore myself. I was drinking more and more of it. So was she. We both drank more and more as the voyage went on. First of all in the evening. Then in the afternoon as well. Then in the morning. Every day we started a bit earlier. There was always some whiskey on board." Drinking fascinates the characters who begin at first for the purpose of physical restoration, then find in it moral security, gaiety and laughter, and wind up forgetting why they have started and not caring much about the reasons either:

"The great drinkers," she said, throwing herself back in her chair and starting to laugh, "they must be incomparably reassuring . . ."
"I should like to be the very greatest drunk of all the southern seas," I announced.
"Why?" she said, laughing.
"Why indeed?" I said.
"I don't know," she answered. "How should I know?"
"How indeed?" I said. "What are you laughing for?"
"Why do you ask me what I'm laughing for?"

But there is a buildup to the strong American drink, a sort of ritual preparation whose ingredients are Chianti, Campari bitters, manzanilla, champagne, and cognac. Counteracting the effect of liquor is a strong odor of coffee: filter, expresso, Turkish; and of coffee houses, sidewalk cafés, but more often and more appropriately, cafeterias. Between the periods of liquor and coffee consumption the characters use a minimal amount of food and engage in sporadic, restless hours of sleep. Above all, and understandably, they complain of fatigue. This is more than physical weariness; it is a lethargic condition that becomes a permanent part of their existence, dulls sensation and emotion, and thus shelters the friendly, acquiescing *victims* from actual participation in life. Finally, there is, as one might expect, very little lovemaking and a great deal of talk about it.

Le Marin de Gibraltar is the story of a civil-service clerk who, for eight years, had been faithfully copying birth records, marriage licenses, and death certificates. Although he does not say so, we imagine that he had always performed his duties with the devotion of a well-lubricated machine and the efficiency of a perfectly programmed computer. Apparently, periods, commas and semicolons were his only gods. Because Jacqueline worked in the same office, and because she was handy and willing, they began living with each other. And because, after the war, people started to move again, to take vacations, to travel, the narrator and Jacqueline join the crowd and take a trip to Italy. But changes in locale and in routine do not alter the makeup of the persons involved. In this connection, the first paragraph of the book merits our attention: "We'd already seen Milan and Genoa and been in Pisa two days when I decided we'd go on to Florence. Jacqueline made no objection. She never made any objection." The word "already" is used frequently by the characters of *Le Marin de Gibraltar*. It matters little whether the action has been completed, is in the process of being completed, or is simply contemplated and has not even begun yet: the personages and the reader experience a feeling of monotony, repetition, and lassitude. There is a lack of enthusiasm, for what the hero does appears to have been done by others, so many times before, and by himself, who knows on how many previous occasions? In addition, wherever he goes he fails to see real differences, for towns are similar, and people resemble each other in spite of arbitrary frontiers. Likewise, the second glass of wine tastes the same as the first, and the tenth would also, were it not for the state of intoxication of the drinker.

Jacqueline, the *objectionless* mistress, makes little effort to shake her lover out of his stupor. She is a timid soul, eager to agree in order to please. Not that she loves the narrator when the story begins. " 'Love,' " he said [an Italian who drives the couple from Pisa to Florence], "is just like everything else. It can't last forever." But it seems as though their arrangement, which lasted *already* for two years, had acquired a certain amount of stability that would have been unwise to disturb: single rooms were, proportionately, more expensive than double, and there was, too, a vague propriety about people traveling together which celibates could not hope to achieve. Besides, she had no objection to allowing him to wait at a café, sipping drink after drink, while she would take in the sights. When, on one occasion, she has the imprudence of insisting that he accompany her to view an Annunciation scene in a local museum, he overstates unabashedly his bourgeois reaction: "I looked at him [the angel] mechanically, without seeing him, my attention concentrated on the relief . . . it was a great relief. My feebleness was leaving me.

I sat motionless and let it go. It was like a man who was dying for a long time to relieve himself, and finally does it. When a man relieves himself he is always very careful to do it as well as possible, to the very last drop. So was I. I was relieving myself of my feebleness to the last drop. Then it was done, and I was at peace." Yet, Jacqueline's escape to the tourist sights in Florence (she visits all the museums and most of the churches in town) is more contrived, for she has little more esthetic appreciation of what she sees than the natural, if dubiously obscene and retaliatory response of her lover.

Actually, what the narrator begins to feel more and more is a mounting indifference toward his mistress. In two years they have run out of topics to discuss, and he, partly because of the liquor, partly because of the torrid heat, cannot even bear to sleep in the same bed with her. In addition, the driver who had taken them to Florence had told him of Rocca, a peaceful fishing village where the yacht of a mysterious, beautiful, and rich American had docked for some time. To escape the heat, the couple goes to Rocca, and it is there that he decides to abandon Jacqueline and never to return to his job as petty civil-service employee in Paris. This is a *gradual* decision, one that he had conceived between two long drinks a while back, at the beginning of the vacation, when he realized that "downing a pint of something or other every hour, life still seemed bearable, worth the trouble of living." And he continues: "I drank, read, sweated, and every so often went and sat somewhere else, changing from inside the café to the terrasse." This *dolce far niente* type of existence appears infinitely superior to copying records. But while his office is far behind, Jacqueline is not. She reminds him of his past, she is the link between him and those dreaded death certificates after the handling of which he "would always wash his hands [until] the skin would become chapped" from excessive washings. No wonder that he begins to think of Jacqueline as of an insect clinging to a hot, sticky body, like "a certain species of red ants, in Mexico . . . that can devour a corpse, bones and all, in next to no time. She looked so sweet, with little teeth like a child's. She had been [my] ant for two years."

The break with his mistress, who leaves immediately for France, is followed by an instant friendship he strikes up with the owner of the yacht. It turns out that she is not American after all; she is French, had married an American who had left her his fortune, and she is now, as she has been for the last three years, seeking a sailor from Gibraltar whom she had fallen in love with, and had lived and traveled with for a brief period. Later he had abandoned her in Shanghai, having gone to a poker game from which he failed to return. Now she is looking for him in all the ports of the world, following the slimmest leads furnished to her by old cronies and ex-crew members in need of money or simply pitying Anna, the perennial searcher of a lost lover. Little does it matter that instead of the sailor from Gibraltar she finds the owner of a filling station in Sète, a swindler in Dahomey. What counts is the endless, quixotic quest, the hope, between whiskeys, that there is something else. Actually, there is very little that Anna has to go by. Her memory of the sailor suggests a number of physical descriptions, and her account of the events which led to their meeting and his disappearance is not always the same. "Sometimes I get the impression that there are ten different stories of the sailor from Gibraltar," the narrator observes to Epaminondas, one of the boat's crew members. But no matter. Seeking gives the illusion of meaning to one's life, and Marguerite Duras seems to imply that the more remote and unattainable the object or person sought, the more significant is the persistence of those who search: for they find continuity and permanence (the continuity and permanence of absence, if nothing else) in what would otherwise be an empty and inactive existence. The following dialogue is of interest in this context:

"And is one allowed to ask what you do?" I asked.
She thought for a moment.
"I'm looking for someone," she said. "I travel."
"Him?"
"Yes."
"Don't you do anything else?"
"No. It's a full-time job."

"The sailor from Gibraltar appears to me to be a symbol for happiness," opined Gérard d'Houville.[31] If so, there is little wonder that Anna cannot locate him, that is that she cannot find happiness in the absolute sense. Small sources of joy to keep one going are, however, available. She is rich, possesses a luxurious yacht, a taste for liquor, and the sailors and other lovers she picks up occasionally (such as our narrator), provide her with a modestly satisfying sexual life. Thus she perceives certain glimpses, certain reflections of felicity. She and the narrator who accompanies her, have become, then, incarnated, have given themselves an aim, a goal. To be sure, at the end of the book they have not progressed much past the point of departure. For in spite of their vastness, all the oceans of the world are nevertheless limited; and there are just so many ports and no more. But there is no limit to the number of times one can travel the same sea or one can anchor in the same harbor. When a cable containing a lead arrives from Havana, there is no hesitation: the boat proceeds to the Caribbean. Anna has been there before but she will go again, responding, "as if to the call of sirens."[32]

Le Marin de Gibraltar has received, for the most part, complimentary reviews. According to Armand Hoog, the author was aiming in this novel, as in the other American-type fiction she wrote prior to it, to arrive

at a definition of existence as Western man experiences it today, in this particular moment of the mid-twentieth century. . . . In modern times, history in its lengthening course has grown heavy, and is charged with and enriched by an increasing awareness. Any contemporary artist worthy of the name knows, or senses, that he is living a fleeting and transitory moment of historic becoming . . . to be explained. . . . The fictional world of Madame Duras is [then] the movement of time, at once creating and isolating personality: the tilting of time toward a past which a second later is transformed into an empty nothingness.[33]

In *La Vie tranquille* there was an invitation to un-tranquil life, to involved existence; in *Un Barrage contre le Pacifique* there was a suggestion of revolution on a social and a domestic level; in *Le Marin de Gibraltar* the theme was expressed by means of the tale of an "absurd, interminable quest, devoid of hope as of despair, of a wealthy woman, traveling about the world."[34] Armand Hoog makes here and in the passage quoted before it a profound judgment on the books of Marguerite Duras, for he stresses the author's astute synthesis of the Catholic, Marxist, Existentialist, and American influences into a clear picture that reveals a historic era, that immediately following world War II.

Perhaps this ability is what another reviewer admired much later in the English translation of *Le Marin de Gibraltar* which prompted the following uncorroborated and surely exaggerated

comment: "Since the publication of *The Sailor from Gibraltar,*
Author Duras has succeeded Simone de Beauvoir as Paris' first
lady of letters, though her novels [since then] have become more
schematic and cinematic."[35] It is well-nigh impossible to determine who the first lady of letters in Paris is at any time, and it
is difficult even to find criteria for making such a determination:
if sales alone are to be considered, by virtue of her more
numerous publications Marguerite Duras appears to have the
upper hand; but she is no Goncourt Prize winner, as Simone de
Beauvoir has been (in 1954, incidentally, two years after the
appearance of *Le Marin de Gibraltar* on the literary scene).
Actually, there were other woman writers in the 1950s, such as
the established Nathalie Sarraute and the more controversial
Christiane Rochefort and Françoise-Mallet Joris, who had
received the lion's share of the reading public's money and
critical acclaim. It is surprising to note, also, that the same
reviewer, while admiring Duras' ability to write "about people
and their moods with incomparable ease and sensuality,"[36]
concluded by saying that we simply "stick with them [the
characters] . . . if only to drink the whiskeys, hear the conversation, and see the sky and the coast as they shimmer from the
yacht,"[37] a criticism which casts some doubt on the permanent
literary validity of the book. This is essentially the opinion of
Gérard d'Houville who likewise points to the rather artificial
atmosphere within which the characters move: "The reader, a
little tired, however, of all these voyages, disillusions and
drunkenness of all sorts, closes the book with a kind of
relief. . . ."[38] But there is no contradiction in the French critic's
judgment, for he starts his review by stating his admiration for
the previous *Un Barrage contre le Pacifique,* in which the author
"remained herself in her singular toughness and her ugly
exoticism," rather than the present novel which "if it did not
bear the name of the writer, we could believe to be an excellent
French translation of an original Hemingway narrative."[39]

It should be added, however, that *Le Marin de Gibraltar,* the
last of the books to be considered under the present heading, and
the most American of the group, is not without its anti-novel
leitmotives. It is surprising that reviewers have not explored these
yet, for they add to the over-all impact of the story. To begin
with, the very theme of a doomed quest that goes on indefinitely,
even after we have read the last page, is typical of the situations

investigated by the authors of the New School.[40] But there is more: the anonymity of the narrator; the changing face and character of the sailor from Gibraltar himself whom no one can recall exactly and who perhaps does not exist; the alcohol-blurred vision of Anna and her traveling companions; the monotony of seas, waves, sun; and the repetitive similarity of dialogues which center mostly on the same person (the sailor sought), on the same absence. Stylistically, there are a number of subconversations, that is, monologues that pass for dialogues, and frequently, too, instances of emphasis on the inability of the personages to communicate logically ideas or feelings. At times, such lack of communication is effectively expressed: "You see," Anna confesses to the narrator, "we [she and the sailor] never said we loved each other. . . . The silence lasted as long as we did. . . . I was full of all the words of love there have ever been, and I couldn't deliver myself of one." The pounding repetition of certain words suggests the limited confines surrounding the characters, the feeling they and the reader get that there is nothing beyond the most counterfeit and frailly constructed means of survival: "I drank two glasses of Chianti one after the other, and waited . . . for the wine to begin to take effect. She watched me drink and she too waited for the wine to take effect. It did take effect." Finally, such pleonastic sentences as: "Epaminondas was . . . of Greek origin," informing us of what we have been told many times before and what is obvious from the name, contribute to the anti-novel characteristics already cited.

These characteristics blend successfully with the American aspects of the tale and make of *Le Marin de Gibraltar* the most widely appreciated example of the writer's initial period of inspiration. The book, transferred to the screen in 1966 by the renowned British director Tony Richardson, with Jeanne Moreau in the title role, reawakened the public's attention to Madame Duras' early work.

V *Summary*

The American-type novel, then, served the author well. Following an uncertain beginning with *Les Impudents,* she was able to include in her next three publications a foreign literary mood and style that post-World War II audiences were only too ready to accept and admire. Moreover, she was equally capable

to hold on, as in *Un Barrage contre le Pacifique,* to numerous
influences of traditional French fiction, and to anticipate, here
and there, the intriguing facets of the anti-novel which was
hardly beginning to emerge on the world's literary scene and
for which she had already a special affinity. The *aficionados* of
fiction who bought her books were provided with a varied, well-
chosen fare: modern and old techniques, poetry, mystery,
descriptions of colonial problems, of life on the farm, exoticism,
the horror of solitude, the consolation of liquor, the pursuit of
love, the loss of love, the fabrication of goals, the all-engulfing
(and for the reader slightly cathartic) absence of a stable, benev-
olent reality sempiternally haunting heroes and heroines. Her
first four novels had revealed in Marguerite Duras a powerful
writer equally at home on a number of topics, an author concerned with her times and our problems, uneven but often
brilliant, pursuing with perseverance and perspicacity a career
that was going to gain her international reputation.

CHAPTER 3

Les Petits Chevaux de Tarquinia – *A Bridge*

I am indebted to Pierre de Boisdeffre for the title of this chapter. In his enormous *Histoire vivante de la littérature d'aujourd'hui* he pointed out, parenthetically, that Marguerite Duras "makes a bridge between the American novel, Hemingway-style, and the New School, with *Les Petits chevaux de Tarquinia* . . . in which the tropical decor and the burning passions of her first books give way to the symbolic beach on which unfolds an abstract ballet of desire and of death."[1] Armand Hoog, too, noted that "after 1953 the manner and tone of her work reach a new level," and he continued: "I should be tempted to see, in *Les Petits Chevaux de Tarquinia* and in *Des Journées entières dans les arbes,*[2] Madame Duras' two perfect accomplishments. The fictional material is here reduced to nothing more than an unfolding and transition, a certain breadth of pure time, without plot, without action as traditionally understood, almost without names (at least without family names)."[3] No writer, however, makes a clear break with the past, and *Les Petits Chevaux de Tarquinia,* as we shall see, still contains a number of characteristics which link it to the American-type novel while it announces, at the same time and unmistakenly, the changing literary interests of the author.

I *Beginnings of the New Novelists*

By 1953 the French novel had already undergone significant mutations. Gone are the glorious days of Sartre: the corrosive action of the human mind appears to threaten seriously both the inner and the outer realities one had been used to. Man, having scarcely escaped from the horrors of World War II and having been engulfed immediately in the new terrors of the Atomic Bomb era, the Cold War, the Korean War and the Algerian War, no longer saw himself in the guise of a conqueror, no longer believed in an unrestricted personal autonomy,

55

in the routines, conventions, and traditions of the twenties, the thirties, and the forties. He looked upon the latter as upon so many traps that denied his freedom and his humanity. More than that, he decided that it was more important to ignore these traps than to fight against them. Thus it was that, gradually, an increasing number of *uncommitted* novels began to appear, raising new questions or raising none at all but rather satirizing those who used to and those who, out of tune with the new generation, still persisted in asking: Jean-Louis Curtis' *Les Forêts de la nuit* (1947), for example, or his later *Les Justes Causes* (1954); Marcel Aymé's sarcastic *Uranus* (1948); the imaginative and picaresque *Les Mauvais Coups* (1948) of Roger Vailland and *Le Grand Vestiaire* by Romain Gary, to mention only a few. There is nothing facile or artificial about these works; they have merely abandoned that great urge to be all-encompassing, to unify, to explain as the Creator himself might, to become a *summa* of man's knowledge and activities. As an editorial in the literary review, *Les Cahiers du Sud*, put it: "The novels of today no longer attempt to set up complete inventories; they no longer present us with an image of complete destruction [or complete creation]."[4]

The stated limitations of the new writers are quite intricate, however, and it is not befitting the present context to discuss them here. Suffice it to point to four basic principles which are reflected, to a greater or lesser degree, in most of their works, as they are in most of Madame Duras' novels written after 1952: (1) Man, in his lucid moments, *knows* that there is no God, no ultimate goal, no absolute meaning; absurdity, therefore, is the underlying fabric of his existence. (2) Traditions, good and bad, customs, conventions and patterns literally strangle Man and squeeze the spiritual out of him; he becomes bogged down in his physical being, he is nothing but a *thing*, an object, a petrified existence: hence, a nauseating feeling of being *de trop*. (3) Because of his ever diminishing humanity, Man is incapable of change, of growth; he is, then, simply an existent in a situation. (4) Man's petrification congeals his thoughts and paralyzes language; therefore, words are inoperative and no communication is possible. It is necessary to stress immediately, however, that this last principle does in no way hamper the writing of novels; it may actually enhance it: "Recounting comprehensible things . . . only serves to make heavy the spirit and to wrap the memory, whereas the absurd exercises the spirit and makes memory work."[5]

Nevertheless, the big publishing houses, scandalized by the writers' attempt to combat the standardized commercial novel and the novel of political and social commitment, refused, at first, to promote their semirevolutionary output. One willing editorial outfit, however, the Editions de Minuit, founded during the Occupation as a clandestine press, accepted the group which was to be known later as "midnight novelists." Samuel Beckett headed the small cluster of budding talent; Alain Robbe-Grillet and Michel Butor were also among the founders. Many worthy books were published by the Editions de Minuit, and soon their increasing sales prompted the better-organized and older publishers to seek the work of the young avant-gardists. Publicity and literary prizes helped their popularity, but what aided also, perhaps more than anything else, were the impressive strides made by the new playwrights.

II *Influence of the Theater*

The avant-garde, more active and more *avant* in the theater, had indeed a considerable influence on the development of the New Novel. The lineage of Alfred Jarry[6] was not so extinct as it appeared, for dramatists such as Ionesco, Beckett, and Arthur Adamov began to assert themselves. Their experimentations of the stage caught the imagination of critics and public alike for they involved a return to Man rather than society, as the center of the dramatic universe. Man was seen as the victim of society, a being exiled from, yet part of the group, a solitude, an island in spite of John Donne and his followers. Unaccepted, he is much like a "bum," that is to say different, in physical appearance and also in spiritual makeup. Hence the cult of the "bum," his transformation into a likable hero, a tragic figure: Kafka's "K" for example, or Sartre's Roquentin. With Beckett, however, the total destitution and misery of the character results in the famous triology *Molloy* (1951), *Malone Dies* (1952), and *The Unnameable* (1953); and on the stage, in the unforgettable Vladimir and Estragon of *Waiting for Godot* (1952). These derelicts are tragic in spite of their comic appearance, gestures, and utterances, for as Estragon says: "Nothing happens, nobody comes, nobody goes, it's awful!" As tragic as they, are also the heroes and

heroines of Ionesco's *The Bald Soprano* (1950) who, their
social respectability notwithstanding, remain strangers not only
to us but also to each other because they are unable to think,
feel, or communicate. There is a lack of order and of logic in
their existence. which they accept and with which they live
quite comfortably.

Thus it is that in the novel also, in the New Novel, writers are
no longer concerned with psychological investigation, with meta-
physical or ethical revolt, or even with intellectual assertion.
These have led, it seems, to a dead end. Now authors become
more concerned with the real essence of humanity, they question what Man is rather than proceed, prematurely, to an explanation of his ultimate goal or even of his immediate aims.
Theirs is a literature of consent rather than revolt, of formulation,
of statement rather than poetic or lyrical interpretation. In 1952,
when Marguerite Duras was busy writing her *Petits Chevaux
de Tarquinia*, Beckett and Ionesco were already gaining a national and international reputation with their anti-plays; and
so was Adamov, whose *Théâtre I*, containing the previously
presented *La Parodie, L'Invasion, Le Professeur Taranne*, and
other plays, was published in 1953; and Jean Vauthier, who had
already showed his *Capitaine Bada* and *La Nouvelle Mandra-
gore* prior to their appearance under the title *Théâtre* (1953);
and Michel de Ghelderode, whose *Théâtre I, II,* and *III* were
made available to the reading public in 1950, 1952, and 1953,
respectively; and others, whose works, too numerous to mention
here, had created an aliterary and anti-literary mood which
spread easily from the stage to the novel.

Actually, in fiction, readers had already seen, before 1953,
Nathalie Sarraute's mysterious *Portrait d'un inconnu* (1949),
Jean Cayrol's triology *Je vivrai l'amour des autres* (1949), *Le
Rempart des Béquines* (1951) by Françoise Mallet-Joris, Jean
Genet's *Oeuvres complètes* (1951-52) containing also his plays,
the touching *Un Jeune Homme seul* (1952) of Roger Vailland,
and many other aliterary publications in addition to the already
mentioned triology of Samuel Beckett. In the American-type
novel of Marguerite Duras herself, we have seen a number
of characteristics which anticipated her liaison with the New
School. These need not be reiterated here; suffice it to recall
how rebellion rarely accomplished anything, how the personages
waited in vain, how they changed with difficulty and only

temporarily, how, often, and after lengthy journeys, they had
wound up exactly where they had started. Her early novels
can also serve to give us a perspective on *Les Petits Chevaux de
Tarquinia*: for they, like it and the fiction which followed, had
their own measure of ambiguity, of terseness of dialogue, of
brevity of line and simplicity of sentence structure which pointed
to the inner nudity and forlornness of the personages; of repetitions and refrains which underscored the tedium of their world
and its interminable futility; of stychomythia, a stylistic device
that satirized the useless attempts at communication between
characters.

III   Les Petits Chevaux de Tarquinia

Marguerite Duras' fifth book fits, then, in the general literary
trends of the mid-1950's. It it, like her subsequent fiction, a longer
short story rather than a novel. There are very few descriptions,
and the rapidity of the almost continuous dialogue would make
it read like a play, were it not for the repetitiousness of the
questions, answers, and statements, and for the monotony and
the slow pace of the action. As in the previous book, the story
takes place in a resort in Italy and, as in *Le Marin de Gibraltar*,
the torrid heat appears to influence greatly the feelings and
acts of the protagonists. Sara and her husband, Jacques, have
come there on a vacation with another couple, Ludi and Gina,
and another woman, Diana, who probably was and perhaps
still is Jacques's mistress. Sara and Jacques have a small child
whom they love dearly, and an impudent, foul-mouthed maid
whom they thoroughly despise. There is another character, a
bachelor, who appears and disappears, the owner of a boat
referred to as The Man and whose name, we learn after about
half the story is over, is simply Jean. He will eventually become
Sara's lover. There is also a nostalgic, chatty local grocer, a
young man who gets himself blown up by a mine (a relic of the
war) and an old woman who refuses to sign his death certificate.
Heroes and heroines sleep, eat, and drink (mostly Bitter Camparis), talk, swim, complain (about the heat, each other, themselves), walk, make love occasionally, and above all vegetate in
a kind of stupor that never fails to grip them from the first to the
very last page. In this semi-dormant atmosphere nothing really
happens. The characters live a *tranquil* life in their villas, or

hotels, or deserted beaches where the unreality of the heat-struck world coincides pointedly with the acute lack of events: "'You're bored? It that it?' She did not answer. 'Is that it, or is there anything else?' 'That's it. I'm bored,' said Sara. 'Me too, I'm bored to death,' he [Jacques] said. And he added: 'What are you bored about?' She got up and tried to smile to him. 'I don't even know any more.'"

Inactivity, when visioned in its extreme, becomes a goal we go after as much as we go after anything else; we seek it actively, we strive for it, we cultivate it once it has been reached. Gina, for example, refuses to go to America where her husband has been called on business, and she often quarrels with him for the sole purpose of effecting a separation that would permit her to lead an even more *tranquil* life. But it is Sara who, more than anyone else, knows the art of making a profession out of boredom. She downs fewer Bitter Camparis than her friends, has a smaller appetite for food and for sex (although she does deceive Jacques on one occasion), and often refuses to go for a walk or a swim. When questioned by Jean on what she does or prefers to do, she answers simply: "Nothing." Actually, what attracts her in him is that he, too, appears to do nothing, go nowhere, and in general foster inertia: "'What do you do?' she asked. 'I have no profession,' said the man. 'That is already a profession,' said Sara."

In order to emphasize better the motionless existence of her characters, Marguerite Duras divides adroitly her book in four chapters, endowing them, in their opening theme, with noticeable symmetry. The first describes Sara getting up late, uncomfortable in the already unbearable heat of the day, going into the kitchen to drink a cup of cold coffee (she never bothers to warm the coffee the maid prepared the night before,) talking sparingly to the child who had awakened first, giving him a shower, then bathing herself, getting dressed, and, having nothing else to do, waiting (for the others to wake up, for Gina and Ludi to come for them and take them to the beach). The beginning of the second chapter sees Sara getting up again, this time from an afternoon nap; it is the afternoon of the same day, and it is just as hot as in the morning; and she proceeds, as earlier in the day, to shower the child, herself, to dress and wait for the others to come for them. The second and last day of the narrative is related by the first few paragraphs of the third chapter: the words used to describe the heat are exactly those used in Chapter I, and Sara makes exactly the same gestures, from drinking her cup of cold coffee in the kitchen to meeting the child on the veranda, to exchanging a few words with him, to giving him a shower, to taking a bath herself, to dressing, to waiting. The second morning is, then, a Xerox copy of the first, and so is the second afternoon which the beginning of the fourth and final chapter recounts: for the temperature is as high as that of the previous afternoon, and she again has to shower the child, shower herself, dress, and wait for her friends. The repetition is not only one of situation but also one of vocabulary: such words as *always, shower, heat, breeze, cold coffee,* and others are found in strikingly brief and similar sentence structures, surrounded by the same articles, prepositions, posssesive pronouns, adjectives, and verbs; and the pathetic effect is exceedingly poignant.

But with all the immobility, the perennial *status quo* of a reality that is too stratified to allow for movement, and in spite of the persanages' refusal to initiate acitivity, a number of insignificant events does take place: the death of a young man who had stepped on a mine, for example, a small forest fire up in the hills, Sara's abandonment to Jean. Calamitous as these events might be to those more directly involved in them, we get the impression that they hardly disturb the dormant, if not dead conditions which prevail. The fire will surely go out when the rains will come, or it will be put out by the local fire fighters; the old woman succumbs and she does sign the death certificate; and Sara, who appears headed to another rendezvous with Jean and perhaps off to the unknown, with him, giving up husband, child, friends, vacation—in a word, routine—Sara has a change of heart. For no immediately apparent reason, certainly not because Jacques knows, or because of any last-minute maternal feelings, or because of any consciousness of wrong doing. Simply because she realizes that there are no revolutions, no adventures, and what happens is only illusory and derisive. She is used to frustration. It is a way of existing, and she will not even run away with her lover with whom she had had a passing, senseless and loveless affair.

Thus, incarnation here will not be simply a flight into the unknown, a break with the past, a vague transcendency of time as in the previous novels. For once it will mean perseverance, not in revolt or in refusal but rather in one's lot, in one's routine, mediocre as it might be. Leaving is not different from staying, and Sara, who persists instead of breaking away, makes acceptable and consoling the very sort of life filled with voids and defeats which she had previously found unbearable. For even this type of incarnation requires a terrible struggle: conquering our unattainable desires, managing to ignore our ambitions and to suppress our vitality, acquiescing in other words in the essential mediocrity of terrestrial existence, means exercising fully our will and, in a way, living. Sara lives now, for with her husband she will agree to go see the equestrian tombs and the *petits chevaux* of Tarquinia—a famous sight that they had heard about, an interesting sight, a modestly interesting sight, that is, hopefully interesting, less dull than their present vacation, perhaps offering a different sort of dullness, one that would not be entirely the same but slightly different, imperceptibly different, different, different. Minute hope is still alive, then, and once the plans for going to Tarquinia have been settled, Sara goes to bed trusting that it will rain in the morning, that the heat will subside. As a matter of fact, *espoir* is the last word of the novel.

Nevertheless, the ordinariness of life remains invincible because it has drained out of Sara and her group all power of true initiative. She and her friends lack the imagination of devising *happenings*, of inventing. Gina, for example, "did not want anything more, except to stay in her room, *tranquille, tranquille*"; the old woman "had become an enormous mass of refusal and incomprehensibility. Without doubt she had decided not to understand any more"; and in so far as the others, as Jacques tells the maid in a speech that is really addressed to his wife and friends: "You have enough of us, and we have enough of you, we are just as sick of you as you are sick of us." What he does not say but is obvious to the reader is that they all have enough mostly of themselves, that they are sick of their own, cumbersome, awkward and superfluous physical and spiritual being. Because such a self-admission would only enhance their misery, understandably, they pick on each other instead: "Ludi and Gina, like themselves [Jacques and Sara] argued a great deal. Long quarrels, without pity, which poisoned the entire seashore, the nights, the vacation . . . yes, petty quarrels on nothing at all, but which poisoned life." And in general, "no one agreed with anyone except in regard to the heat." In a vague sort of way some of the personages realize, at times, what is missing: " 'What is it we lack?' Diana asked. 'Perhaps the unknown,' Sara said. 'In this place we are completely cut off from the unknown.' " Thus, waiting for the unknown becomes the ideal occupation. Only mystery turns out to be always recognizable, always an object of derision. What is left, therefore, is waiting, "for each other, every day," and waiting, too, for everything, so that "in order to decide whether or not to take a swim at noon one of the women said, you had to start thinking about it at nine in the morning, to ask everyone, as soon as you got up, in order to find someone to go and take a dip with you. This because each waited for another, another other than himself who the night before had promised to swim with you but, since, had promised the same thing to someone else. It was a web of reciprocal waiting, without end."

IV *Summary*

Les Petits Chevaux de Tarquinia may be said to be one of Marguerite Duras' best attempts at fiction. Her pen is no longer that of a beginner: it has gained assurance, audacity; it has learned how to position and repeat words[7] in order to create the unmistaken mood of desolation that she wishes to impart; it has perfected, above all, that ability to combine a number of characteristics of the American-type novel with the touching, crushing but nevertheless still cathartic facets of aliterature. As we view the world of Bitter Camparis, that society devoured by the solitude of togetherness and the boredom emanating from uneventful events, we are prompted to weight our own participation in that world, to measure carefully the exact position we occupy in it, to relate our ennui to that of Sara, our frustrations to hers also, our desires and our hopes as well. Marguerite Duras' novel can thus be viewed as an awakening agent, a springboard to lucidity. And even the most placid reader is bound to be affected to some degree.

CHAPTER 4

The Anti-Novels

I Des Journées entières dans les arbres

THE year 1954 sees the publication of Marguerite Duras'
first work to have practically no connection with the conventional novel form. Actually the book is a collection of four
titles: *Des Journées entières dans les arbres,* the only one that
is longer than the average short story and which could be
considered a brief novel; "Le Boa"; "Madame Dodin"; and "Les
Chantiers." *Des Journées* has attracted a considerable amount of
attention, especially in its play version of 1966 under the adept
direction of Jean-Louis Barrault and benefiting from the experienced play-acting of Madeleine Renaud. All four titles, however,
are good examples of almost plotless compositions pursuing the
vein of the New Novel through repetitions, anonymity of characters, and infrequency of incidental detail. Yet, as we shall see,
the author does not make a clean break with the past: summaries
are still possible; the totally dismal atmosphere of the masters
of the New School is absent; and false, awkward hope still
glitters, from time to time, in the heart of the personages.

The nostalgic connotation of the words *des journées entières
dans les arbres,* pointing as it does to children climbing trees
for the joy of pure ascension or the intriguing mischievousness
of discovering bird nests, fills the one hundred or so pages
of the first story. There is a touching feeling of loss that grips
the reader immediately, to stay with him and grow as the almost
continuous dialogue of the composition unfolds, cryptically at
first, but more and more plainly as the narrative advances. The
loss is, of course, that of the days of old, the carefree days, the
moments of sheer innocence, of play. And the void that we are
left with is only poorly filled by tangible objects, by material
riches that we have grown too old to enjoy or even care about.

For that is the situation of the central character, the nameless
mother who returns from the Colonies to see her son, Jacques,

a middle-aged man, a boy who had liked tree-climbing, frolicking, and playing hooky from school, a boy who had not quite grown up yet in spite of his chronological age. It is this son among all others whom his mother loves and whom she comes to visit, perhaps because she senses that he needs her, or perhaps, as one critic has put it, because she wants "to assure herself that he had not come out of his infancy, that is to say from a sort of biological slavery"[1] that she could still, secretly, enjoy. This mother, unlike Ma of *Un Barrage contre le Pacifique,* has done well abroad; she has become the proprietor of a factory and has acquired jewels, bracelets that she wears on every arm, and rings that cover almost all her fingers. Her son, on the contrary, has not changed very much. He is lethargic, sleeps all day, and at night he dances with old, single women in a nightclub where his concubine, Marcelle, has a somewhat similar job. Moreover, he is a drunkard, a gambler, a thief on occasion (he steals some of his mother's jewelry the one night that she sleeps in his apartment, in order to sell them and gamble with the money); but he is also a gay sort of man, capable of passion at times, sensitive and childish, a dreamer whose degradation has a measure of voluptuousness, for it is willed without being calculated. His is a world of inactivity and consent, perpetuated and cultivated with care, much as that of Sara and her friends in *Les Petits Chevaux de Tarquinia.* In vain, his mother offers him status and fortune in the Colonies: "This is the way he is," the same critic pursues, "and this is the way he will age, oh bitter and delicious victory of this woman who has come so far and who has not quite gotten over the *treason* of her daughter (did she not dare to take a lover and break off with the family?), who uselessly hides her thirst for domination and often does nothing but think passionately of her own person."[2]

In *Des Journées,* Marguerite Duras' pen excels indeed. Her penetrating analysis of the three main characters—mother, son, and mistress—almost exclusively by means of dialogue, is masterfully handled. The author's descriptive interventions are reduced to the minimum and are never more than a few lines long. In this story, just about every spoken word has an intense, a pounding, dramatic value, as if the pen were that of a playwright and not that of a novelist.[3] "I am always hungry," says the mother almost as soon as we meet her. "Night, day, always

. . . I am so hungry and thirsty." These statements, repeatedly made, act as a refrain and they constitute but one example of the writer's ability to bare immediately the psychological makeup of her personage.[4] How neatly, then, her jewelry-studded hands fall into place, and the twenty-room house she owns and boasts about but has no real use for, and the factory in which her eighty employees are busy making her a fortune that she does not quite know how to spend. Yet, is hers a hunger of money for the power, the freedom it provides? Not really. Rather for the *things* one can buy with it. Things, to be sure, not quality: had she any real appreciation of jewelry, for example, she would purchase and wear items of a more expensive and subdued character. Hers is also a hunger of much smaller, more animal needs: a *choucroute*,[5] which she eats heartily, on several occasions, during the short visit she pays her son, a glass of Beaujolais. "Oh, the joy that a *choucroute* gives," she exclaims at one point. "No one knows it so much as I do. A good choucroute . . . and I passed my seventy-fifth birthday . . . two wars . . . when I think of it . . . in addition to everything else."

Her apparently disconnected but closely knit aberrations point, of course, to the infirmities of old age, to the decay humans are subjected to prior to death. She hears with difficulty, for example, does not see too well either, and is unable to think coherently or to recall except through the fluid opacity of a septuagenarian. The little that she says is replete with contradictions and reveals an unstable personality whose sensitivity only serves to enhance the pathetic quality. She is much like other aged characters of the masters of the New Novel and the New Theater, Ionesco and Beckett for example, a decrepit individual, physically and intellectually in an advanced stage of decomposition.[6]

In a different way the plight of growing old is also visible in the son: for while he has aged, he has not matured; he still leads, essentially, the carefree existence of his tree-climbing days. And it is visible in Marcelle, too, for she, the moving symbol of a cheated life (abandoned by her parents, raised in a loveless atmosphere, caught in the facile web of prostitution because of necessity, laziness, or both), of love erased by time, of an ardent desire for something different, for a pulsating life which would not be threatened from all sides, which would be devoid of fear, hunger, and uncertainty, she has also forgotten how to look to the future; she has consented, has acknowledged and accepted, that dubious state of survival into which so many of Marguerite Duras' personages sink. For her, as for Sara, the status quo is not only possible, it is desirable because the unknown could only be worse: she might lose her job at the club, she might become ill, Jacques could leave her. She must be constantly careful, then, at work, in her conversations with the mother, in the way she dresses and exhibits emotions. In the play version, the reviewer aptly noted her "naked face, an imperceptibly hesi- tant walk, shaking hands, a pale mouth pointing at the same time to her tenderness and ferocity, and a voice, finally, pure, trembling, tense, calm, ironic, light: barely anything, yet theater at its best,"[7] for the actress' appearance and tone, changing and conflicting, denote so well the permanent inner struggle which the author wished to convey. As a matter of fact, the dramatic qualities of *Des Journées'* descriptions and dialogue lend them- selves so effectively to stage production that the reputable Chris- tine Garnier has been moved to remark: "Gripping author, admirable actress: one does not know, upon coming out from the Odéon,[8] whom to praise more. Madame Duras or Madame Renaud? Our heart is seized, we are fascinated, we know that the magic will last *des journées entières.* . . . Madame Marguerite Duras, we know it already, is a great writer. We had liked the tone of her famous novel, *Barrage contre le Pacifique,* and the unusual dialogue she wrote for Renais' film, *Hiroshima, mon amour;*[9] but perhaps nowhere better than in these *Journées entières dans les arbres* did she know how to unveil the chiaro- scuros, the moving sands [of human relationships] and to im- press us with [mere] somnambulists."[10] Yet, *Des Journées'* pages remain the pages of a novel. They never become exercises, dra- matic or otherwise, and if we agree with the conclusion of Armand Hoog that "Marguerite Duras has written nothing better,"[11] it is in the novel itself that we must seek the clues to its bewitching interest.

The starting point could hardly be simpler: a mother returns to visit her son after an absence of years. The visit will last approximately twenty-four hours, during which the characters will talk, eat and drink, go to the club where Jacques and Marcelle work, return home, sleep, get up. Nothing will really take place. If the son steals, gambles, and loses, he simply con-

firms an early reader's anticipation; and the very few paragraphs
that these events occupy do not give the plot any movement.
What impresses, what touches, is the dialogue: the unfinished
sentences, the brief, concise, incisive, staccato utterances, the
alogical apostrophes, the curious interpolations, the sad and
moving expressions of disenchantment and despair of the
personages:

"Tell me a little about your life, the two of you . . . make a
little effort."
"Always the same," said the son.
"Truly?"
"Exactly the same," the son repeated.

To the familiar theme of immobility is added, repeatedly, the
devastating proof of an aging person's decaying reason and loss
of memory: "Yet, in general, your father and I . . . I am not
saying now. . . ." She stops, seeks to recollect: "We had rather
kind sentiments one toward the other."
The Existentialist's nausea is likewise an integral part of the
story: "Here I am thinking of all those men in my factory. It
comes back to me as a feeling of nausea. . . . As a feeling of
nausea . . . I don't know why." Much like the engulfing roots
of the tree in Jean-Paul Sartre's La Nausée causing nausea in
Roquentin's stomach, the recollection of her material possessions
brings about a distasteful, physical reaction to Marguerite Duras'
character. But unlike Roquentin, she is unable to reason out the
origin of her response, nor does she have the intellectual or
physical drive to seek even the shadow of a remedy.
The painful realization that in real life contradictions are
frequently compatible, a theme often encountered in anti-
novels,[12] and expressed frequently in Des Journées, adds to the
intriguing qualities of the dialogue: "It's the same thing after
all . . . to work . . . not to work, it's enough to start, to take on
the habit," says the mother, trying halfheartedly to convince
Jacques to follow her to the Colonies. As a matter of fact, all
three main characters contradict themselves often and are awkwardly unaware, at the time they speak, of what they have said
a few moments before. Thus, the mother's affection for her son,
the apparent reason for his visit, becomes a mere conjecture
when she admits: "If I am here it's because it was the thing to
do, because I told myself that my duty was to come see my son,

to attempt again the impossible. . . . nothing more, a question of duty, but my heart is over there [with her men and her factory]"; she says this in spite of the fact that before, repeatedly, she had expressed scorn for riches, had commented on the too many rooms in her house and the too many workers in her factory and the excessive sums of money she had but was too old to use.

Finally, the protagonists' inability to pursue a topic for more than a few lines, their wandering mind and instability, their subjectivity and egocentricity are admirably pointed out by the author through the characters' vain efforts at real communication, at understanding. For although the story is almost exclusively made up of dialogue, *Des Journées* contains nothing more than subconversations and long monologues, interrupted, broken, hesitating, dangling. There are many which could be given as examples, but one of the most moving occurs in the episode in which Mother and Marcelle begin to talk on a subject of common interest, Jacques, then each revert, from time to time, to purely personal preoccupations while apparently continuing the conversation:

"I even think that I love him," she said.

The mother, hearing these words, trembled.

"He doesn't, he never will love me."

But the mother was once more off to the spectacle of her dancing child.

"Besides, he tells me so. Never will he love me, never, never."

Mother looked at her, examined her without seeing anyone.

"He never wanted to go to school," she said, "never. Never. It all stems from that. That's how it all began."

"And why not?"

Mother's hands flew out in a gesture of impotence.

"I don't know it yet, I shall never know it."

They remained quiet for a moment, then Marcelle dove back into her own preoccupations.

"If only he would let me stay with him, I'm not asking for anything else, just to let me stay."

"There are children, the others for instance, who get by all by themselves, no one has to take care of them. With some, there is nothing to be done. They are brought up just the same, they have the same heritage, and they are so different."

Marcelle remained silent. The mother remembered she was there.

And the monologue-dialogue goes on in unaltered fashion,

the two women talk mostly to themselves, only sporadically recalling the presence of the other.

Des Journées is also noteworthy for the brilliant stylistic sallies of the writer. Only an attentive page-by-page reading could do justice to the mysterious allusions, the intriguing repetitions, and the *choucroute* stench that emanate from Marguerite Duras' pen. Consider, for example, the sadly ironic words of the mother who, speaking of other children, of those who have made a real place for themselves in life, quips: "Oh, they have studied, have had jobs, got married, just as children gulping jam or something." Or the regret she expresses for not having been wise enough to enjoy the *good old days*, the days when she was poor financially but rich in health and in children: "She touched her arms, felt them as one does some vile merchandise. Nothing anymore, she went on. No more children. No more hair. Look a little at my arms. . . . Nothing more except for that factory. . . . When I think, and I can still see you, when I think that you were all sleeping like angels in all the corners of the house . . . in the shadow of the blinds, green, do you remember? . . . And I cried just because I had some debts. To think that you were there and that I was crying. . . . Alas, my breasts bulging with milk, strong like an ox, and I was crying." Or the epilogue of the well-constructed scene at the nightclub, when the mother refuses to pay the bill on the grounds that she was overcharged for the little she has drunk, and the crowning remark she makes after she does pay: "It's almost as expensive as a mattress, how odd," pointing to an association between drinking and abandonment to sleep or death, a subtle, engaging association which surely originates in her intuition only. Or the profoundly poignant reasons she gives to Marcelle for leaving so soon after her arrival: "If I go, you see, it is because it doesn't even seem that I am here . . . not at all . . . not at all. To have had children, it has no meaning, it means nothing. Nothing. You cannot imagine to what point all this is insignificant, it's enough to make you dizzy. I don't mean to have them . . . but to have had them. . . . If I remained, he could only kill me, the poor baby. And I, I'd only wind up understanding him."

This is the most feared thing of all, of course, for then she would lose him entirely; he would become like the others, all of one piece, predictable, sane, safe: he would no longer be in a state of "biological slavery," and she, as the mother of an infant, would cease to exist. In one of her last speeches, guarding against this possibility, she remarks: "If you knew . . . the others [the other mothers] . . . they are proud of theirs, and when they come to visit, what do they see? A bunch of bourgeois, animals, too well fed, and dumb, not knowing anything. No my son, I am proud that you are like that, still like that at your age . . . skinny like a cat . . . my darling." What she does not realize is that she does understand him after all, even more than her other children, for with him her intuition is her wisdom, and she can feel and display a host of emotions that she is incapable of in the case of the others. In her penultimate speech, this realization comes to the surface, porous for the reader but certainly still opaque to her own declining intellectual capacities: "Mine is another pride, and I am the only one to understand it. And I only suffer, my darling, because I am the only one to understand it, and because I am thinking that I shall die and that no one, after me, will ever feel this type of pride." It is obvious, then, that her haughtiness is not pleasurable because it cannot be shared: with the exception of her son, she could ill afford to show it to anyone else. It is, as she says, more a source of pain than of joy. Moreover, were she to stay close to her son for a longer period of time she would run the risk of seeing him change, hence of losing the lofty position she now appears to have. Therefore she must leave the only person she can dominate, resume the total loneliness of the Colonies and assent to distance, absence, and death.

In *Des Journées*, then, three unfortunate people — mother, son, and mistress—spend part of the day and one night together: hardly the material for a novel. We find a great deal of dialogue, though, a limited number of precise details: barely enough even for a short story. Yet, the world of the dispossessed is admirably described, the complexity of contradictory emotions is conveyed with touching sensitivity, and the loneliness of immobile characters who accede to their miserable situation is perfectly identified. Perhaps not a novel, these *Des Journées*, perhaps not even a short story. But Marguerite Duras is here too close to reality to aspire to lesser goals.

II *"Le Boa"*

The second title in *Des Journées entières dans les arbres* occupies only sixteen pages. Unlike the first, "Le Boa" contains very

little dialogue. It is a first-person brief memoir of a woman
who looks back to the time when she was thirteen and she
attended a school for girls whose directress, a virgin septuagenarian, had admitted her out of pity for her mother who was
too poor to pay the full amount of the tuition.

Mademoiselle Barbet was at worst vicious, at best eccentric.
While the other students were permitted to go out every Sunday,
to the movies, for walks, to play tennis or otherwise amuse themselves, the narrator was subjected, each week, to two unvarying
spectacles: a boa devouring a chicken at the local zoo, a free
show which allowed the directress to charge her pupil's mother
for "Sunday outing" expenses; and, upon returning to the seclusion
of the school, the ugly nudity of the old woman who forced the
girl to watch her undress so that she could boast about the
quality of her underwear. These two unusual weekly events
acted upon the mind of the young girl with almost catastrophic
consequences, although her present ability to review them logically, clinically, points to the absence of major damage on her
personality.

The intuition of the child told her that the boa's killing and
assimilation of the chicken was a pure, innocent act, and that
her directress' exhibitionism was the embodiment of mature vice
brought about by the frustrations of virginity. Marguerite Duras'
description of the first Sunday occurrence is a blend of ferocious
cold-bloodedness and poetic admiration. The spectacle of the
boa's feast moves her character to remark:

What an impeccable crime, consumed in the warm snow of its
feathers which added to the innocence of the chicken a fascinating
reality. This crime was without stain, without a trace of spilled blood,
without regret. The order after the catastrophe, the peace in the
chamber of the crime [the boa's cage]. Entirely curled, black, shining
with a purer dew than that of morning on berry bushes, of an
admirable shape, a swelled roundness, tender and full of muscles, a
black column of marble . . . replete with shiverings of contained
power, the boa was integrating this chicken in the course of a
sovereignly lofty digestion, as perfect as the absorption of water by
the burning sands of the desert, a transubstantiation accomplished
in sacred tranquillity. In a formidable interior silence the chicken
became boa. With a happiness to make you dizzy, the flesh of the
biped was flowing through that of the reptile.

By opposition, the sight of Mademoiselle Barbet's nudity fills
the forced spectator with scorn and disgust:

> She would keep herself erect so that I would admire her, bending
> her eyes to look at herself lovingly. . . . It was too late. . . . A terrible
> odor emanated from the body of Mademoiselle Barbet. . . . I would
> stop myself from breathing. Yet, she had her own sort of kindness.
> And in the whole town her reputation was secured, perfect, as
> virginal as her life. I would tell myself that, and also that she was,
> after all, an old woman. But it didn't matter. I would still stop myself
> from breathing.

In the child's mind, then, violence meant purity and virginity
signified vice. To guard herself against the possibility of winding
up like Mademoiselle Barbet, the narrator would go to the
window and smile to passing colonial soldiers, much like another
Duras heroine,[13] in the hope that one would stop and kidnap
her and rape her and save her from the horrifying infirmity of a
sexless existence. More than that, she began to suspect the *good*,
and to feel limitless sympathy for the dispossessed, the villain,
the *evil* in society. Confessing that she had heard only much later
about the commercial side of prostitution, she then tells of her
vision of a bordello "as a temple of defloration where, in all purity
. . . girls . . . who were not destined to get married [because of
a poor financial background], discovered their body with the
aid of unknown men of the same species as they. A sort of
shrine of impudicity, the house of prostitution had to be a silent
place where no one spoke, everything being so arranged that
no word need be pronounced in its sacred anonymity." And she
pursues: "I imagined that the prostitutes put on a mask on their
face before entering. Without doubt, in order to earn the anonymity of the species, the absolute lack of personality of the
boa. . . ."

It is useless to wonder whether the narrator, who ends her
story in a beautifully poetized vision of her future,[14] should have
been more prompted to choose the path of the boa than that of
Mademoiselle Barbet. This piece makes no pretense at plot or
credibility. It merely points, with simplicity and sobriety, to the
workings of the mind of a young girl under the imperious fatality
of two events imposed upon it from the outside and viewed
now from the vantage point of maturity. It suggests, of course,
the very little choice a child has in the difficult process of grow-

ing up and of shaping a personality: for while not everyone con-
templates a boa devouring a chicken, nor smells the decaying
body of a naked septuagenarian week after week for a number
of years, other similarly uncontrollable forces mold and petrify
human life. This is a pathetic consideration, especially when
made (perhaps only intuitively) by a teen-ager. Yet, Madame
Duras' approach prevents "Le Boa" from becoming a soap opera
type of narrative. Her introduction of the developing feelings
and ideas of the girl remains, throughout the brief pages of the
story, cautious, medical, a bit too calculated perhaps. We are
left with the impression that what we have before our eyes is
not fiction at all but rather a well-studied case history. That the
author could have accomplished this in spite of the many poetized
passages points to the writer's ability to weave in a brilliant style
even the most ludicrously violent events to have been described
by her pen. Perhaps nowhere is this more apparent than in
"Le Boa's" last paragraph:

Thus the world, and therefore my life, opened up on two avenues
which gave me two distinct alternatives. There existed, on the one
side, the world of Mademoiselle Barbet, on the other, the compelling
world, the fatal world of the species considered as fatality, the world
of the future, luminous and burning, singing and shouting, of a deft
beauty, but to the cruelty of which one had to accede as one had
to accede to the spectacle of devouring boas. And I would see that
world pointing to my future, the only possible future for me, I would
see it opening up with the music, the purity of a serpent's unfolding
body, and it seemed to me that, when I would come to know it, it
would be in this way that it would appear to me, in a development
of mystic continuity . . . with movements of terror, of enchantment,
without rest, without fatigue.

But a woman is not a boa, and for most young ladies the fascination of the bordello decreases with maturity. It is quite probable,
then, that Marguerite Duras' narrator, who never mentions a
family, or a husband, and who confesses having learned, eventually, of the commercial side of prostitution, never did attain the
serenity and innocence of the serpent. Did she become another
Mamedoiselle Barbet, or was she simply afraid, at the time she
began to recollect her childhood, that her emulation of the old
directress was an inevitable prospective? In either case, the
reincarnation that the young girl had dreamed of, as she smiled,

naïvely, to passing soldiers, appears to have struck the older woman as a fanciful utopia she could only look back to with a mixture of nostalgia and cold-blooded lucidity.

III   *"Madame Dodin"*

The two husbands Madame Dodin had had were drunkards. She had left them both. . . . [her children,] she did not want to see them, they bored her. She had given them a fine education . . . and for them she had worked in a factory for fifteen years. In the evening, her earnings not being sufficient, she would take in other people's washes.

"I worked so much for them," she explains, "that I've had enough. All I ask is that they leave me alone."

But the *others* hardly ever leave anyone alone, and Madame Dodin, caretaker of a modest apartment building, is even less in a position to aspire to the peace and quiet due a tired, old woman.

One of the duties to which she objects constantly is the daily chore of emptying the tenants' garbage cans. She has done it for years, of course, every morning of every day of every week, but she has complained about it all day, every day of every week, to tenants, to neighbors, to a street-sweeper whom she befriends, Gaston, to anyone who would listen. Specifically, she detests the odor, the weight, the contents; generally, she is bothered by the servitude that emptying other people's garbage suggests, her relegation to a position of inferiority, her intuition that, somehow, her chore reduces her to a subhuman. In her impasse, Madame Dodin, too lucid and too experienced to hope in the accepted sense of the word, cannot be aided by faith or by revolt: "God is nothing to brag about," she says, "I'm telling you. And then, the Son, just as bad as the Father . . . and the Communists, they're just like the priests, except that they say they're on the side of the workers. They repeat the same thing, that we've got to be patient, so there's no hope from them either." Dispossessed as she is, what is left for Madame Dodin to do? Not very much, not much more than other Marguerite Duras heroines have been able to devise: she unravels old pull-overs, for example, and she talks a great deal. Not that she does anything with the wool or that she says anything when she speaks. Her remarks are nothing but clichés: "The sky is heavy

. . . there is going to be a storm." Or else: "The sky is clear,
it's going to be nice for the rich." But although she lacks both
faith and the ability to revolt, she has not quite given up. Her
daily complaints keep her busy, alive, and give her a measure
of significance which keeps her one step above the garbage-can
type of existence she leads. But there is more: she refuses to
go to church, as a friend suggests, for that would mean accept-
ing the idea of patience, of compromise with the present for
the sake of an illusory future; she has visions, at times, of
impossible solutions, such as "special sewer openings in which,
everyone, each night, would be compelled to empty his garbage"; she has a certain passion for Gaston, with whom she
laughs, quarrels, perhaps even goes to bed; she is not above
stealing, on occasion, the home deliveries of the tenants, and of
boasting about the thefts; finally, and more importantly since
the wish is made part of the last paragraph of the story, Madame
Dodin looks forward to dying with a certain sadness but also
with satisfaction if, death coming during the night, there would
be no one to empty the trash cans in the morning: "It's a pity,"
she often says, "I won't be there to see their face."

Gaston, the male counterpart of Madame Dodin, only thirty
years old (she is sixty), is no different in spite of his younger
age. She empties garbage, he sweeps it. As if he were already
quite old, Gaston works slowly, walks painfully, his head bent,
his broom dragging behind him, paying attention to no one
(except, occasionally, to Madame Dodin), and is almost always
indifferent, anonymous, alone. He drinks, he gets fat, he is a
picture of progressive decay: "He has lived too long . . . the
people in the neighborhood can die or take their First Com-
munion, nothing moves him. He is no longer interested in human
ends. They bore him. . . . And in all the human joys or mourn-
ings he perceives nothing but gradual deterioration." Because
he is younger, the unchanging monotony of his work appears
even more pathetic. Old or young, Marguerite Duras seems to
suggest, the routine and the dirt of the subhuman functions
which we must all perform to a greater or lesser degree, make
life barely bearable and inconsistent with our more beautiful,
more fanciful visions of it. For like his friend, Gaston too
dreams: "What I need is 20,000 francs. To go to the South, take
in the sun and maybe, who knows, get another job." And in this
ideal location he would stop working at four in the afternoon,

he would be free, he would be known, people would shake his
hands, he would take part in conversations, he would meet a
girl, a brunette, she would smile to him, he would smile back.
There is nothing much in the meantime, however: three glasses
of white wine a day, the daily exchange of banalities with
Madame Dodin, the possibility, quite vague and certainly
meaningless, of a physical relationship in a moment of stupor
or drunkenness.

Both Madame Dodin and Gaston, then, lead the existence of
previously met Duras characters: theirs is a miserable life,
a human condition they are unable to change. Yet, increasingly,
they become used to it, and only in moments of removal from
reality are they capable of imagining something better. These
moments are sufficient for survival, however. They guarantee a
trace of security, they reincarnate humans into a more humane,
more acceptable situation. More than that, in "Madame Dodin"
the author inserts some of her rare humorous passages, at which
readers laugh with, and sometimes more than the protagonists:
the old woman's way of *kidding* Gaston by emptying, on him,
from her window, her pots and pans; and Gaston's impatient
wait, under the window, for Madame Dodin to appear and to
splash him with the contents of her kitchen vessels. Some of
the conversations between the two are particularly comic,
notably the one in which Descartes and philosophers in general
are taken to task for theorizing about matters that are too
remote and of no immediate value to the masses:

"It urinates, therefore it drinks," Madame Dodin said.

"This reminds me of something," Gaston noted. "A philosopher
said the same thing: I think, therefore I am."

"He would have done better to keep quiet," Madame Dodin said,
"if he didn't discover anything better than that."

"The one who discovered it was Descartes," said the street-sweeper.
Madame Dodin burst out in laughter.

"What kind of cards? As far as cards go, I only know about ration
cards . . . with all their brains . . . why didn't they find something
to do away with garbage cans?"

Unlike Beckett and other anti-novelists who use humor efficiently
to point to the tragic side of the human condition, Marguerite
Duras takes advantage only rarely of comic devices, and the
passage quoted is the lightest to be found in her publications
to date.

But "Madame Dodin," in spite of its aliterary aspects which place it in the larger context of Marguerite Duras' ties with the New Novel, and in spite of the fact that it points to an unsuspected, though sparingly used ability to handle jocularity, has not been, so far, the object of critical comment. Like "Le Boa," it has been eclipsed by the success obtained by the first story in the collection, *Des Journées entières dans les arbres*. Yet, "Madame Dodin," and "Le Boa," are carefully written compositions suggesting unmistakably the mature pen of a novelist whose talent will result in books of increased and permanent literary value.

IV *"Les Chantiers"*

Positioned last among the four short stories under discussion, "Les Chantiers" does not appear to have the gripping qualities of the first three. In it Marguerite Duras plunges into the New Novel (as a matter of fact, it is barely possible to speak, in this instance, of a mere connection with it); yet, as we shall see, the ending of the brief narration constitutes a sudden and unexpected ascent from the world of the despairing and the dispossessed, and what had started as a deeply pessimistic relation of the impossibility of human communication and relationship winds up in a syrupy, semi-Hollywood type of denouement.

She and He, guests at a resort hotel, meet outside of it, in front of an enclosure where an edifice is about to be built. There is nothing remarkable about either protagonist, and their anonymity coincides with their lack of luster. As does the reader, so do She and He notice the average in the other: the plain physical appearance, the lack of excitement of their movements, the slow pace of the daily routine in which they engage. Vacation here, even more than in *Les Petits Chevaux de Tarquinia*, is synonymous with stagnation. Whereas in the previous work a number of events did take place, and dialogue was at least apparently possible, in *Les Chantiers* the characters are unable to exchange more than a few words, and whatever microscopic action there is, it remains locked in the mind of the personages. He, for example, takes more pleasure in observing her furtively than in talking to her or in establishing a more tangible rapport. She, on the other hand, ignores for a while that she is being watched and proceeds with the mechanical activities of her vacation: the meals, the walks, the aimless entries into and exits out of the hotel; and when she becomes aware of his silent attention, like him, she makes a subconscious effort to avoid a meeting and to check the possibility of verbal intercourse. These subconscious attempts become more conscious later on, so that the two are able to hold on to that more subtle, more pleasurable feeling derived from indefinite waiting periods and from vague but passionate and unfulfilled desires.

In the man's case at least, the *happiness* he experiences is purely intellectual, and he soon begins to lose appetite and the ability to sleep; for it is eminently difficult to wait everywhere for a woman one hopes would never appear; and to watch everyone of her gestures without being seen and without making the interest visible to her or to others. In addition, the sight of the slightly soiled collar of a blouse she wears one day awakens in him a sexual image that leads to the discovery of more potent reasons for postponing the development of a real friendship:

The view of this collar dirtied and wrinkled by this neck, this back of her neck half hidden under her hair, that material [of the collar], these things that he alone saw, that she did not know he saw . . . it was as if they were two to live in this body she had . . . [and] the night which followed that day the memory transformed itself into desire . . . but this desire was immediately so strong that he wanted her to be even more ignorant than she was of the life which was taking place within her [ignorant of his participation in that life]. Thus, once successful in possessing the woman he would be able to get hold of her more fully, to take advantage of her entirely, to dispose totally of this body whose sovereign negligence he had been able to uncover.

There is, then, no reason to force or to hasten an acquaintance-ship; there is every reason to savor the delicious misery of waiting.

Or is there? The tone of the writer in *Les Chantiers* does not favor a precise conclusion. While she describes at length the protagonists' mysterious joy in the highly sophisticated game of hide-and-seek they play, she also appears to mock their *vie tranquille* (the words are repeated several times in the story and they recall, of course, her 1944 novel of the same title), the way He "plunged slowly, each day, more deeply into the red forests of illusion," the actual pleasure he feels when she passes by without recognizing him, his secret wish that she leave the hotel and his silent enumeration of all the reasons she might have for leaving, his refusal to stop her in the street and talk to her, his equally emphatic decision, "No, at the risk of losing her I would never strike a conversation in public," and, finally, "the absence of drama in his life." But over and above the derision in which she holds, perhaps, her characters, Marguerite Duras, in typical anti-novelist manner, does not fail to point with sober sensitivity to the tragedy of their condition. The few banalities which she has them exchange, not about themselves but about exterior, unimportant things (comments on the building under construction, on the men who work on it, on the changing landscape), reveal beyond doubt the emptiness of their existence. Their nervous gestures too, their forced smile and occasional laughter which "expressed neither irony, nor confusion, nor coquettishness but only a certain incertitude," their extreme care "to ignore one another as if, in this resort hotel, in the middle of the summer and in spite of their freedom love had been condemned to death," unveil brutally the personages' marginal participation in life. He and She have everything going for them, and there are no outside impediments to the birth of love. But contact beyond the mere trivial and the briefest moment is impossible since there is no inner drive, no initiative, no desire to satisfy desire. There are only certain glimpses, a number of material, solid objects (the bricks and mortars and ropes the men work with, for example),[15] and the strangely consoling catharsis to be derived from them: "When she left again . . . the man felt like calling her back and shouting to her that this was a chance, a joy, the existence of things such as the fence around the enclosure inside of which the men were working. He did nothing of the kind. He could neither cry out to her to stay, nor could he get up in order to try and hold her back. This impotence was also mysteriously satisfying."

The very idea that satisfaction can result from a deficiency points to what extent Marguerite Duras adheres to that literature of consent mentioned in conjunction with earlier works. But unlike before, in Les Chantiers she adheres to it until the very end (or almost), and the reader has no advance notice of the possibility of even a modestly happy outcome. In a very tight structure, untainted by the slightest suggestion of sentimentality, the author appears to endow her characters with such petrified qualities of timorousness, timidity and reserve that we seem to deal more with some Beckett or Ionesco-type personages than with the more malleable, more flexible protagonists we had encountered on previous occasions. In the shorter format of the *nouvelle,* we are led to think, there is very little time for He and She to engage in any sort of liberating act which would insinuate at least the appearance of a closer rapport. Besides, He and She find, increasingly, a curious fulfillment in desire without satisfaction or in satisfaction derived from incongruous sources. That is why, when at the end of the story the two meet abruptly, at the edge of a forest, after a long walk in the course of which she had followed him with mechanical precision, we are unprepared and unwilling to accept what is obviously a contrived conclusion. The characters, it seems, had tasted such extreme pleasure in waiting, and had experienced such intense emotions in deliberately vain efforts at contact that we now view their encounter as anticlimactic if not as a non sequitur. The reader who has allowed himself to be drawn into the rhythm and tempo of the story sees himself suddenly outside it. Events which had appeared to him to lead to an essentially negative outcome in line with the characters' makeup take a turn away from the inner truth of the situation, and an artificially happy ending is constructed at the expense of the stated limitations of the personages' ability and desire to make contact. The meeting in *Les Chantiers,* the back cover of the 1967 French edition informs us, "is the story . . . of the first beginning of love." That love can still begin after most of its emotional intensity has been experienced and consumed is as dubious a hypothesis as is the future of the now united couple, facing one another, without comment, fresh out of words (the inner dialogue has used them all) and of feelings too (He and She had waited too long, had met too often before they actually met).

The fact that Marguerite Duras ends her narrative with the unexplored union of hero and heroine points at once to the necessity of keeping within the boundaries of a short story and to the impossibility of going beyond the mass of internal reactions which had fatigued and weakened the characters. Thus, the sugar-coating of the denouement is not prolonged by sentimentality or emotional fakery. This, of course, is to the credit of the writer who will not, in the future, depart so radically from the circumscribed and limited status of the initially described reality. That she had, in a story more closely connected with the tenets of the Anti-Novel than any other, remains without explanation; unless it be that in *Les Chantiers* she felt suddenly that she had gone too far in a direction that she was not prepared to accept fully for fear of seeing her own, very personal fictional potentialities conform exactly to those of a semiestablished literary school. Madame Duras' integrity clashed, perhaps, with the writer's domination of plot and characters, and the writer lost. But *Les Chantiers* does not occupy a prominent place in the author's fiction. Except for the usual reviews concomitant with the publication of all her books, it has not given rise to critical comment. Marguerite Duras can easily afford to charge her last story to experience and emerge, as she will, in stricter control of subsequent literary endeavors.

V Le Square

A man and a young girl happen to be sitting on a bench in a public park. The man is not doing anything. The girl is looking after a little boy playing somewhere nearby. A simple word concerning the child, and thus begins a dialogue between the man and the girl. The child wanders around, comes back, asks for his milk, goes off again, and comes back once more. Darkness approaches. The girl leaves with the child. Nothing has happened. A novel has been born.[16]

Marguerite Duras' seventh story provides an excellent example of the author's ability to exercise tight control over plot and characters. Since its publication in 1955, *Le Square* has been a favorite work with critics and public. To my knowledge, only one reviewer has had reservations about it,[17] all others having lauded the narrative in unmistakenly complimentary terms. In France its popularity has resulted in a most successful stage version in 1960, and in this country the book has had many editions, among them an annotated one destined for intermediate college students of French and quoted above.

The plot of *Le Square* is perhaps as well known to the American fiction reader as is that of *Hiroshima, mon amour* to the moviegoer. A detailed résumé is not necessary here. Suffice it to point to the unusual conversation between two persons meeting on the neutral ground of a park bench, and to the fact that it alone constitutes the novel. As the author has done for *Des Journées entières dans les arbres,* she relies on the strangely haunting quality of simple words and uncomplicated syntax to

weave a pattern of human existence: the similarly empty life
of a young girl, a maid, and that of an older man, a traveling
salesman of shoelaces and razor blades and other such petty items
people usually run out of, from time to time. Who are these
individuals, mysteriously drawn toward one another, from about
4:30 in the afternoon until the fall of darkness? We know neither
their name, nor their age (the girl says at one point that she is
twenty-one, at another that she is twenty-two, and she might
be either or perhaps she has no idea how old she is; the man is
ten, or twenty, or thirty years older than the girl, but the text
is of no help in determining his age), nor exactly what they look
like, what they hope, or why they feel a mutual attraction. But
we do know that a bond is born out of the clichés and the repetitions of the dialogue: the allusions to concrete, everyday situations, the associations, the questions, the unfinished phrases
reveal to each the awkwardly formulated sensitivity of the other,
their latent, inner moods, and the urgent need to break the bars
of solitude and escape into the world of communication, of
assertion and recognizable identity.

Yet, there is a marked difference between the efforts the man
and the girl are able or willing to sacrifice to their objectives.
His temperament is more one of consent and resignation. He
resembles the characters of *La Vie tranquille* before the murder
of Jérôme: he has not chosen yet, has not become incarnated.
Struck by the platitudes and trivia of daily living, he awaits,
he does not know what, perhaps for something to happen, something terrible and catastrophic that will provide his elusive
raison d'être. But he is and feels too old to hope that the future
might still have something for him. It is easier to consent to
the present, as Sara and the others had done. Only once he did
not do so, only once in his life had he felt like dying, that is
only once had he been fully aware of his existence. And the
experiment did not appear worth repeating. The lesson that he
had managed to teach himself was that an accepted predicament
is no predicament at all, and that "the lowest of the low," as he
considers himself (and the girl he is speaking to) can vegetate
along, peacefully, once all other recourses have been exhausted.

On the contrary, the girl finds herself in a *live* impasse. She is
a simple, naïve domestic constantly abused by her masters who
overwork her because they sense that she is not capable of
resistance. But for her there are no short cuts: she refuses to

make her labors easier even when the opportunity presents itself, for to do that would be to become reconciled to her situation. In the past she had attempted to: she had gone to inquire at the office of the Maids Union if some of the jobs she was required to do, such as that of taking care of a senile, enuresis-ridden old woman, could be properly assigned to her; and she had thought of killing the octogenarian, which would have been easy, because she was old and unloved by the family. But she had found out that the union could not do anything, that in effect there was nothing in its code about such things,[18] and besides, if she had elected to quit her job there would have been ten other girls who would have jumped at the opportunity to replace her; and in so far as the assassination idea, she tells her interlocutor: "Not only I do not do it, but I even take better care of her, for all the same reasons I have already mentioned, namely because, if I did kill her, it would mean that I envisage my situation as vulnerable to amelioration, briefly, as bearable . . . this would be contrary to my plan."

The maid's deliberate refusal to exit, whenever possible, from the difficult situation in which she finds herself (by changing households or killing the old woman) can be linked to Jean Genet who, in his own life and many of his works, expressed a similar desire to reject the idea of ameliorating his condition.[19] "It is because it is intransigent that her despair is constructive," Claude Morhange Bégué opined cryptically,[20] but Jean-Paul Sartre first, and in a much more lucid statement had explained Genet's unusual reaction which inspired, perhaps, that of Marguerite Duras' personage: "He could not be content to accept abjection as a temporary and contingent effect of circumstances: that would have meant resignation. In order to conserve the initiative and because others were the makers of his misfortune, he had nothing left to do but to carry his misery to the absolute."[21] Only the maid in Le Square carries her misery to the absolute sporadically and on a temporary basis. Understandably, she has less stamina than Genet and most of his fictional characters. Not only has she tried in the past (with the union), but all along she had devised and carried out, as far as she could, a plan which would change her status as outcast, as a debased sub-human.

What is this plan? She states it clearly: "Only a man can make me get out of it, neither the union, nor I." And it is here that lies the main difference between the two characters in the book. The woman has a plan, an idea of a future unlike the present, a future encompassing a home, a family, a husband. She wants to be chosen, that is, not to incarnate herself or become incarnated merely with the help of an anonymous group of outsiders such as the union; her wish is to be selected by another human being whose love or need of her would erase permanently the stain of her condition as servant, as "the lowest of the low." In this respect, she shows as unacceptable and too simple Sartre's contention that a person can and should acquire his own essence through personal, unaided efforts.[22] For she does not envision mere social justice; what she wants is a full metempsychosis into a person of honor and dignity. Her hope is, then, infinitely stronger and more specific than the vague and unfulfilled waiting with which the man contents himself. The girl's imagination and bourgeois taste make her less intemporal than her temporary friend. But what is ironic and cruel is the fact that her hope is not based on reality, for she is too shy and to a degree too resigned herself to make true efforts toward the realization of the dream. Her weekly attendance at a dance, so far, has not netted her the attention of any man. Yet, her simple, stubborn return, each Saturday night, in search of a dancer who will want to become interested, is sufficient: she will exist until she will be able to live, fully aware that "nothing has yet begun for her" but confident that something will begin.

And at the end of the story we see a faint possibility of a reunion, a vague possibility to be sure, more in the mind of the woman than in the will of the man, but a possibility nevertheless. "Perhaps then we shall meet again this coming Saturday" is the last sentence the maid addresses to the traveling salesman. "Perhaps, yes, perhaps. Good-bye," he responds, and we wonder if he is to be the domestic's future husband, if she will become the bridge which will take him across from hibernation to life. We do not know the answers to these questions (although we suspect they are negative), nor are we left with a feeling of frustration when we turn the last page of the book. For the story is complete such as it is, not merely the chance meeting between two lonely hearts, as it might have degenerated into the hands of a less skilled writer, but a revealing dialogue replete with psychological undertones and engaging interest. And then, too, we remember well the lesson of *La Vie tranquille*: marriage constitutes a utopian incarnation, for the mediocrity of life will sooner or later grip the couple and unleash the dehumanization process temporarily stopped. Maybe it is just as well that the heroine holds only a faint hope of meeting once more her interlocutor of an afternoon. For who knows if *it is better to have loved and lost, than never to have loved at all?* As for the hero, his acquisition of an identity at any cost, not through heroic and significant acts but through a gesture, a formula such as that involved in a marriage ceremony, constitutes an end perhaps not worthy of the lonely torpor in which he now finds himself.

In *Le Square* Marguerite Duras appears to have come to terms with the old problem of creating characters who achieve an emotional intensity and unity going beyond the limits of the outer events related. These, held to the barest minimum and uncorroborated by the author's descriptive interventions, benefit effectively from the strict control mentioned above and evident in the carefully written verbal exchanges between the couple, in the accuracy of the nuances they express, in the restrained images they evoke, sometimes in the sober richness and timid sensuality which dot the conversation; that is, in *themselves*: in the truest and most painfully explored fibers of the speakers. Thus, the girl is not a mere example of a whole class of servants, overworked and abused since the beginning of time, in dire need of an official investigation and of proposed measures to alleviate the thorny social problem they pose; he is not the paradigm of the lonely traveling salesman, removed from society by the nature of his profession, a nomad who has forgotten the art of establishing ties with other human beings. "Marguerite Duras," the reviewer of the play version states, "does not [merely] *come to realize* that little maids are solitary, silent and sad [persons], she *experiences* herself the weight of their solitude, their silence and their sadness which crush in particular the poor girls and [other] deprived individuals. The great works of objection and revolt do not describe what happens to a class of beings especially eroded, they express what happens to each of us, to the author first. . . ."[23] Under the writer's pen the girl and the man remain entirely subjective, *themselves*. This is a particularly touching aspect of *Le Square*, for it emphasizes the very personal qualities of characters who, refusing to speak and feel for all the others in their class, speak and feel for *me*.

The beautifully delicate balance achieved between the maid

and the traveling salesman should not be viewed, then, as a mere esthetic accomplishment. Theirs has not been an exchange of Truth but of truths. They did not fake conversation and did not pose for each other. Their approach was honest, full of integrity. And the fact that they, "the lowest of the low," have been able to reach a measure of understanding, untainted by sentimentality or deprecation of or recoil from truth, suggests a cathartic quality which forces the attentive reader to participate, to become an accomplice: he exits tremulously out of his own closed world of insignificant solitude and steps, with care and hesitation, into that universe discreetly poised between the light and the darkness of the afternoon, between that indifference and (im)possible birth of love evoked in words which translate familiar emotions, well-known impulses, and intimate reactions. How far Marguerite Duras is, in *Le Square*, from earlier novels such as *Un Barrage contre le Pacifique*, in which the writer's interference and outspoken preachings detracted, to a degree at least, from the purely literary validity of the works.

That is why it is difficult to agree with Armand Hoog's assertion: "As soon as Marguerite Duras decided to establish herself opposite, beside or on the frontier of the abstract novel, things began to go a bit wrong. . . . *Le Square* is an admirable tour de force, but Marguerite Duras will not succeed it twice [sic]."[24] To begin with, the author had been flirting with the New Novel for a long time, and *Le Square* appears to be a natural outgrowth of earlier tendencies maturing and kept under a masterful control. Moreover, the label "a tour de force" does not take into consideration the writer's concern, in this novel, for essentially human emotions which appeal even more than the unusual bittersweet dialogue of the composition. Germaine Brée, in her brilliant introduction to the Grove edition of *Le Square* and three other novels by Marguerite Duras points to some of these "stark, basic human emotions; desire, dread, suspense, solitude, happiness, as they pertain to one basic ocean of feeling for others, which is love." And she adds: "Love, the fierceness of love, the happiness, the pain, the compelling and destructive power of love is Marguerite Duras' essential theme"[25] —and not just in *Le Square*, but as the critic notes and, we shall attempt to show, in most of her subsequent books as well, which contradicts, of course, Armand Hoog's later contention that the story under discussion "represents an interlude rather than any evolution in the work of the novelist."[26]

VI   Moderato cantabile

Three years after the publication of *Le Square* appears the very short (sixty-five pages in the Grove edition mentioned above) narrative of *Moderato cantabile*. It is noteworthy that only once before (the six-year period between the appearance of *La Vie tranquille* and *Un Barrage contre le Pacifique*) Marguerite Duras has taken a longer time to complete a book, and that, since 1958, no more than two years have elapsed between publications. Apparently, in spite of its brevity, this carefully written composition required an expanded period of concentration on the part of the author.

Armand Hoog, in whose opinion *Moderato cantabile* is not a real anti-novel but, as he cryptically states, "a novel which hesitates, which falls back upon itself, a hesitating novel, undecided and perplexed,"[27] considers it paradoxical that she should have gone with it from Gallimard to the Editions de Minuit, headquarters of the New School. It is curious, however, that the critic's article on Marguerite Duras appears in a special number of the *Yale French Review* entitled "Midnight Novelists." But more about this later.

As John W. Kneller has observed,[28] *moderato cantabile* is to be interpreted as an antithetical term which is never used for a musical composition: the directions usually specify *moderato* by itself or in connection with *allegro* and *andante* in order to qualify the meaning of the single word; *cantabile*, which means "singable," points to a group of notes that are to be sung. *Moderato* is viewed by the same critic to signify the routine and restraint imposed by habits and by society on the novel's principal character, Anne Desbaresdes, while *cantabile*, on the contrary, is to be interpreted as the temptation, on Marguerite Duras' heroine, of ultimate freedom, of involvement, of love and violence, of metempsychosis.

The two themes unfold admirably in the brief novel, from the very first scene and through the eight chapters into which the story is divided. The author manages to create immediately a tense drama between a stubborn child, a bored mother, Anne Desbaresdes, and a stern piano teacher, Mademoiselle Giraud, whom the pupil cannot or will not obey. Largely through dialogue, Marguerite Duras succeeds in evoking a powerful inner-outer struggle. There is nothing between the three personage-enemies in the room but an indirect contact, a bond of chance. Miles separate the characters: the child goes through the motions of playing the piano, automatically and badly; the teacher insists on technicalities which are meaningless in terms of the pupil's early development of method; and the mother appears to despise her unbearable and indocile offspring. Actually, twice in the novel (once to her boy and later to a man, Chauvin, whom she will meet) she remarks that, often, she thinks she invented her son, that he does not really exist.

As the music lesson proceeds, with quiet, poetic humor Marguerite Duras points to the dramatic distance between the protagonists: the child's attention to the noises outside (of the sea, of the motorboats) and to the beauty of the sunset ("The child, motionless, his eyes lowered, was the only one to remember that dusk had just exploded. It made him shiver."); the teacher's harsh reprimands but obvious lack of interest and charity; the mother's secret pleasure in the obstinate refusal of her son to learn, to conform, which she associates with her own stifled desire to escape the conventionality and humdrum of an empty existence as wife of a rich industrialist, on vacation at a remote seaside resort. To the teacher's persistent request for an explanation of the meaning of *moderato cantabile,* the boy's ignorance, feigned or real, points, for his mother, to the possibility of eluding the routine and the monotony of her life. *Cantabile* "fights" *moderato* outside of the apartment also, for while the bickering goes on inside, a murder takes place in a café across the street. And the cry of the victim, of the gathering crowd, of the police sirens insinuates itself into the room, into the inner fibers of the three personages, like a terrible and inescapable obsession. Anne is most afflicted, for while others live and die outside, she waits and is bored and has no hope of participating in real human dramas.

Across the street the killer has been arrested, and the crowds have dispersed. No one knows exactly why the murder took place. Rumor has it that assassin and victim were too much in love. When the police arrived, the murderer stood over the body of the woman, his lips grotesquely chained to hers, her blood spotting the collar of his shirt. Anne goes into the café and meets

Chauvin, one of the workers in her husband's factory. He had witnessed the murder and now attempts to satisfy Anne's curiosity about the details. As they speak, they are mysteriously attracted to each other, and they will meet, day after day, in order to drink and talk about the crime that had taken place. There is, of course, no real reason for their clandestine meetings. The simple explanation which they share at first, and which becomes more and more difficult to accept as time goes on, is that Anne must know the motives behind the murder and that Chauvin hopes to dig into these motives and relate them to her. But pressed continuously by questions, he soon runs out of details. He does not recall very much about the case, he has not been an attentive witness. "I'd like to know a little more," she keeps repeating. "Even if you're not sure of your facts." So he imagines how the *others* must have met, how their relationship must have developed, what they could have spoken about. Anne becomes intoxicated with the personality of the victim, she cannot help mimicking the gestures and movements the other woman must have made, or repeating the words she must have said, in the intonation she must have used. Her identification with the *other* is her incarnation, her participation in life, in the mystery of life, in the happiness and violence of life. Little does it matter that Chauvin, too, begins to play; that his role is that of the killer; that their perusal of the game of unbearable passion the *others* must have gone through can only come to one predictable end: Chauvin, the assassin, will have to kill Anne, the voluntary gull. But when Chauvin raises his hand and utters: "I wish you were dead," Anne responds simply: "I already am." His gesture is useless, for the woman has already discarded *moderato* and has chosen *cantabile* in its place.

Or has she? The choice is not certain, although it appears that the answer is in the negative. If we place *Moderato cantabile* in the context of Marguerite Duras' previous novels we cannot escape the fact that, for most of her characters, incarnation remained utopian. Becoming someone else, finding identification with another, are not simple operations like that of forging a passport. And the flimsiness and sketchiness of Anne and Chauvin do not point to the strong will required for the complete process of metempsychosis. Actually, what do we know about hero and heroine? We know that she is intrigued by or falls in love with Chauvin; we suspect that he is intrigued by or falls in love with

Anne. But the psychological adultery in which they engage does not go past one dubious kiss in the café. And if "they lingered in a long embrace, their lips were cold and trembling . . . performing . . . a mortuary ritual." There is, of course, the much-acclaimed regurgitation scene of chapter seven, when Anne, arriving home late for a reception scheduled by her husband, goes through the hostess' motions poorly, eats the *saumon glacé*, the *canard à l'orange*, and the mocha ice on top of the many glasses of wine she had drunk before, and winds up vomiting "the strange food that had been forced upon her." This scene, interpreted by John W. Kneller as symbolizing "the end of the conventionality theme,"[29] the abandonment of *moderato*, does not make up for the fact that Anne's love for Chauvin was lived only emotionally, that there was no love affair as such, and no actual murder. In spite of the five confrontations with Chauvin, in spite of the wine and the almost accidental kiss, the heroine has remained herself, the bored, lifeless Anne who had been mimicking the *other* who was indeed assassinated because she had been alive, really alive, and because she had kindled in her husband, or lover, or whatever he was, a passion or a hatred or a madness that is only possible with the living. Likewise, in spite of Chauvin's perseverance and efforts in trying to satisfy Anne's curiousity, in spite of his emulation of the assassin's gesticulations and phraseology, he too fails in his attempt at incarnation: he does not succeed in possessing the wife of his boss, nor in killing her. And his last attempt at reaching for the woman's neck is as futile as the kiss in which their icy lips had met when he had tried, vainly, to give to their relationship the aura of passion that the other couple must have known and enjoyed.

The relationship between Anne and Chauvin proves only that an alienation from society is possible, for a short time, and that the strictures and restrictions of bourgeois respectability can be avoided without permanent danger by those rebels who repent and return within the orderly mechanism of accepted decorum. Just as the child learns eventually the meaning of *moderato cantabile*, so do hero and heroine discover the futility of stubbornness, of contradiction, of revolt, as evidenced in their final separation. However, their capitulation and consent are in no way inconsistent with the short-lived adventure and imitation of the *others*. The latter played a major role for they rekindled in the protagonists an awareness of the existence of other dimensions, other values, other rules: extralegal, violent, fiercely relentless and almost within reach. This newly acquired cognizance is sufficient to make them go on, to survive. Thus, it may be said that the unnamed town in *Moderato cantabile* is no different from Tarquinia. In both places, a number of calamitous events took palce, but even those most closely connected with them could only be touched temporarily. And characters who had attained an elusive poetic presence, a kind of purity and eternity in another, a different and forbidden world, realize that *moderato* alone is a practical sine qua non of the human condition.

The incompatability of the two musical themes of the title is beautifully interwoven in the narrative pattern. Nowhere is this more obvious than in the seventh chapter, with its description of the formal dinner scene inside the house and the relation of Chauvin circling the mansion outside the garden railings. Anne is painfully aware of the double role she must play as respectable hostess, trying desperately to behave according to the norms of the society within which she lives, and as frustrated woman prey to the stark sexual and destructive desire which she feels welling within her for the man whose nearness she guesses with every fiber of her inebriated being. An object of scandal to husband and guests inside, an object of wild passion to the man prowling outside, Anne moves and speaks with hesitation, uttering fragments of sentences and restating with every gesture and every word the dichotomy that is within her until she vomits both the wine she had drunk earlier and the socially acceptable victuals of the gala dinner of which she had been forced to partake. All this corresponds pointedly with the sonata form[30] which is usually divided into three parts: exposition, development, and recapitulation. Two opposing themes, in this case *moderato* and *cantabile*, unfold through these stages and end in a *coda* or closing theme, in the present novel the act of vomiting. But Anne's regurgitation is neither an acquiescence in the invitation to freedom of *cantabile* nor, for the time being, a return to the security of *moderato* (it is only after the fifth meeting with Chauvin in the eighth and final chapter and following her inability to become in actuality a victim and his to become in actuality a murderer that the separation will take place); it is, in its simplest interpretation, an expected physical reaction on the part of a person that has had too much wine to drink and too much food to eat. But it is also an indication of the heroine's utopian incarnation, for while the salmon, the duck, and the mocha ice are her husband's, the wine, which is also ejected, has been bought for her by Chauvin. To see in her temporary ailment a proof of definitive metempsychosis is to be taken in by the tragic modulations of the finely controlled musical themes and to forget that no absolute emulation has taken place, for after all there has been no actual consummation of love and no actual murder.

Excellent control is evident not only in chapter seven but in the novel as a whole. For example, Marguerite Duras is extremely careful about her chronology; all episodes take place at the same time of day, the first begins on a Friday; the fifth, sixth, and seventh on the following Friday; the eighth two days later. The entire plot unfolds in clearly delineated sets, all positioned between late afternoon and evening. Control is likewise apparent in the author's use of verb tenses. While most of the composition is written in the narrative past, we are fully aware that the action takes place in the present, and the illusion of the past only serves to enhance the sense of immediacy of the situation. In the dinner scene of chapter seven there is an unexpected shift to the present tense in order to make absolutely clear the urgency of the rapidly moving events that will culminate in the vomiting incident. But the act of spewing itself and the rest of the chapter are written in the future, as if to cast additional doubt on an already complex climactic scene. Finally, there is a return to the narrative past in chapter eight, as befits Anne's and Chauvin's impending reversion to *moderato*, the inescapable solution.

The enthusiastic reception accorded this novel can be explained also by the writer's continued interest in the stylistic devices of the New School: the broken, interrupted conversations, the repetitions, the lack of specific details, the alcohol-blurred vision of the personages through which the reader must interpret the development of plot, to an extent the anonymity of characters (we learn Chauvin's name very late in the book, and those whose names we know from the beginning remain vague, sketchy, and wanting in completeness), finally, the cinematographic technique of set construction, not unlike that of Alain Robbe-Grillet's *Last Year at Marienbad* (1961), to which *Moderato cantabile* has already been linked.[31] Much of the dialogue is also in the tradition of the New Novel:

"I meant to ask you, you're not working today?"
"No, I need some free time for the moment."
"Time to do nothing?"
"That's right, nothing."

Recalling a somewhat similar exchange between Sara and Jean in *Les Petits Chevaux de Tarquinia*,[32] the passivity to which this passage points is often under the protagonists' attack during their encounters. To guard against it, to make it less visible to each other, she asks question after question and he attempts to respond, as best he can, inventing when he no longer knows what to say. But periods of silence sneak up on them just the same, and they find their awkwardness unbearable. At one point he pleads: "Hurry up and say something. Make it up." And she reacts with a long speech, without punctuation, in the film version declaimed by the actress almost in one breath: "People ought to live in a town where there are no trees trees scream when there's a wind here there's always a wind always except for two days a year in your place don't you see I'd leave this place I wouldn't stay all the birds or almost all are seagulls you find them dead after a storm and when the storm is over the trees stop screaming you hear them screaming on the beach like someone murdered it keeps the children from sleeping no I'll leave." Lack of communication and the inability to agree on even the slightest matters are likewise continuously pointed to. In this connection, Marguerite Duras appears, on one occasion, to recall another passage from *Les Petits Chevaux de Tarquinia* when she writes: "Some people declared that the day had been hot. Others ——and they were the majority—did not deny it had been a beautiful day, but claimed that it had nevertheless not been hot. Still others had no opinion."[33]

It is clear, then, that *Moderato cantabile* belongs as much to the New School as did *Des Journées entières dans les arbres* and *Le Square,* as will all of the author's subsequent fiction. "On page 77 the man who was simply The Man can no longer persist in anonymity," observes Armand Hoog. "'I am called Chauvin,' he says. How that little sentence pleases me! I have confidence in Marguerite Duras. She is a great novelist who will rise superior to the perils of the literary *school* [the Anti-Novel school]."[34]

Outside of the fact that, eventually, we learn Chauvin's name, and that Armand Hoog appears to have philosophical reservations on the merits of the anti-novel, it is difficult to see how *Moderato cantabile* can be interpreted as the beginning of a return to traditional fiction. The books which follow it deny this. And if Madame Duras rises superior to the unspecified perils of the New School, it is because she does not follow to the extreme its abstract, disintegrated, and often cold-blooded themes; because her personages remain essentially human in their preoccupation with the problems of solitude, of communication, of desire and love tempered and frustrated by social deliberations; finally, because they rebel against the subhumanity to which they are frequently relegated, and because they fail and they consent to it, as tragic heroes and heroines do once the glossiness of revolt is erased with the passage of time.

VII Dix heures et demie du soir en été

Marguerite Duras' talent for applying cinema techniques to novel-writing is especially obvious in her next fiction publication. About *Dix heures et demie du soir en été* Germaine Brée commented: "The story of Maria's night of anguish and revelation is told in an atmosphere of intoxication and nightmare, visually reconstructed as in a film, each moment sharply etched in darkness or light, without any recourse to explanation, extraneous comment, or moral judgment."[35] Actually, the novel was made into one of those "new-wave" motion pictures in 1965, at a time when Marguerite Duras' popularity in the United States had reached the dubious point of netting her *Vogue Magazine* assignments and write-ups. The film enjoyed excellent reviews, as did the book itself, one of the best to have been penned by the author.

The plot of *Dix heures et demie du soir en été,* built, as in *Moderato cantabile,* around a murder unwitnessed by the central character but intensely felt and relived by her in the course of the narrative, proceeds along a clearly suspenseful trajectory positioned in time between the semidarkness of early evening and through the pitch-blackness of night to the shiny, radiant sky of the next torrid day; such a trajectory lends itself, of course, to the dramatic effect of changing lights on the cinema screen.

Stopped by a summer storm on their way to a vacation in
Madrid, Maria, her husband Pierre, a friend, Claire, and the
couple's daughter, Judith, are forced to seek refuge in a village
off the highway where the lack of electricity and adequate hotel
accommodations promote an immediate feeling of uneasiness
growing in intensity with the turning of almost every page. The
intermittent downpours, the electrical discharges, and the onslaught of the stranded travelers on the only hotel available,
complement artfully the police hunt for Rodrigo Paestra, the
native killer who, having caught his wife in the arms of another
man, implanted death on both lovers and became guilty of
murder after having been guilty of no longer being loved.

"Rodrigo Paestra," the villagers keep repeating, in tones varying from admiration to recrimination. "Rodrigo Paestra" echo
those who search for him, the would-be avengers and the
entire town's police force, those who pursue him in the streets
and those who track him down on the village roofs, relentlessly,
passionately: for he who has violated the peaceful serenity of
the inactive and the unconcerned must pay with his life for the
crime of audacity he has committed.

The haunting cry of the assassin's name has a special impact
of Maria. This woman, embarked on her husband's vacation, not
her own, this wife, whose friend and spouse have fallen in love
with each other, feels, suspects, and ultimately knows that for
her, as for Rodrigo Paestra, a crisis of catastrophic proportions is
about to come to an unavoidable conclusion. For she, like him,
is being pursued: the others' desire had reached out to her during
the all-day drive, and accompanies her now, in the bars where
she seeks refuge, in the streets on the way to the hotel, in the
dining room and at the table where she eats and drinks with
them. It is no longer possible to ignore the lovers' uncontrolled,
mute, but visible and authoritative sexual attraction; and Maria
has no recourse but to recognize it, to submit to it, and to accept
it with humility and with freedom from personal rancor with
regard to husband or rival. As a matter of fact, convinced and
overwhelmed, she acquiesces to Claire's superiority: "In the
candlelight, her beauty was even more obvious. . . . Claire, this
beautiful fruit of the slow degradation of their [hers and her
husband's] love. . . . Maria became aware of Claire again, and

of Claire's beauty which nearly made her cry." But there is
more than lack of recrimination and admiration of rival; there
is deep personal suffering, moving and pure in the heroine's
efforts to reconstruct the others' birth of love: "In what part of
the hotel, did they first wonder and marvel at having known each
other so little until then, at the wonderful agreement that had
grown between them, and then at last come to light . . . behind
this window? or on that balcony? or in this corridor?" In maso-
chistic fashion she observes the progress of love and the growth
of the others' sexual desire, and her manzanilla-tainted mind
does not prevent her selflessness from almost being sorry that
"love hadn't been fulfilled that night in the hotel," that there
was to be "more waiting. The rest of the night." More than that,
the sight of Claire, "as she waited to be coiled up against Pierre,
that night, in Madrid, naked, in the warm moistness of a room
closed to daylight, when Maria would be asleep in a lonely
slumber brought on by liquor," awakens in the heroine a feeling
of sympathy not usually encountered in the abandoned and the
deceived. Actually, when the hotel clerk in Madrid assigns couple
and rival adjoining rooms, she is even prompted to think with
regret of the interfering role she would accidentally be made to
play for "Claire, tonight, in the fulfillment of her desire, would
not be able to scream." It is clear to everyone, most of all to herself, that, as Marguerite Duras points out, Maria "had accepted
defeat forever."

The central character of *Dix heures et demie du soir en été*
furnishes, then, still another example of a protagonist of the
literature of consent mentioned before. Little does it matter that
an attempt at action, at complicity and involvement, at incarnation, has been made when she had tried, in the middle of the
night, to save Rodrigo Paestra from the fate awaiting him.
Her gestures: motioning to him to allow himself to fall off the
roof on which he was hiding into her car, driving him outside
of town, depositing him out of sight and promising to return
next day and take him across the border, are suspenseful, dramatic, cinematographic sequences, doomed, we suspect, because the police are still around, because Maria might not be
able to persuade husband and rival to help her carry out her
plan, because the assassin himself appears to have lost interest

in escaping, in living. As a matter of fact, there is little surprise when, in the morning, she discovers Rodrigo Paestra's corpse in the field where he was supposed to wait for her, his body bathing in the blood dripping out from the self-inflicted gunshot wound. We find once again Utopian incarnation, acquiescence in the impossibility of contact as well, and proof of the extreme vulnerability of all human beings. Thus, Maria will go on with the others to Madrid, will return to the ineffectual substitute of the mother-daughter relationship, to her glasses of manzanilla, face to face with death, that glamorless void of the end of a futile adventure. "What can we do?" she asks of her husband in the last page of the novel, knowing full well that there is no answer to her question. And when he tries to comfort her with lies, the following touching dialogue ensues, pointing admirably to the heroine's docile lucidity:

"It's the end of our story," Maria said. "Pierre, it's all over. The end of the story."
"Be quiet."
"I'll be quiet. But, Pierre, this is the end."
". . . Are you sure?"
She said she was.

Yet, the consent and the choice of passivity involved in giving up her husband are balanced, to a degree, by Maria's encounter with Rodrigo Paestra. He, like the heroine, is a person dispossessed, a reprobate, a person banished, removed from society because his wife fell out of love with him just as Pierre fell out of love with Maria. "Rodrigo Paestra is [also] a murderer," Jacques Guicharnaud commented, "hence . . . the most fallen, thus the purest of men." And he added: "At that level understanding is possible, whether experienced by physical desire or by language, or by both. At that level the search for another is worth the trouble to be considered . . . but even then it does not necessarily come off. . . . Maria sees her adventure elude her because Rodrigo remained solitary and chose, without her, to kill himself."[36] For a while, however, for an instant poetized and romanticized by the storm and the brutal, primitive surroundings, the Spaniard's crime demonstrated to the French heroine that mutiny was not a mere illusion, that it was a possibility, a very real door that the unafraid and the proud could push open in a moment of liberating madness. But the self-annihilation of Paestra slams shut that door, and Maria once more becomes convinced, this time permanently, of the futility of effort, of opposition, of rebellion. She knows, with a stubborn, physical awareness, that all is over between her and Pierre; that the words *the end* circumscribe and stop brusquely the relationships between human beings; and that there is no escape except in stripping oneself of the derisory habit to will. Like Sara of *Les Petits Chevaux de Tarquinia* (with whom she shares a gusto for drinking and an abhorrence of heat), like The Man of *Le Square,* like the couple in *Moderato cantabile* and a host of other protagonists, Maria bows, concedes, "accepts with resignation those fatal laws of time and of human passions"[37] to which the lucid always ultimately succumb.

The most banal of stories, the infidelity of one spouse toward another, is molded by Marguerite Duras into a powerful Romantic-Classic setting in which, according to Germaine Brée, "outer and inner events fuse, merge, and develop with a poetic inevitability."[38] The setting is Romantic because of the lightning, the thunder, and the persisting rains; it is Classic because of its brevity (the entire novel takes place in less than twenty-four hours), because the plot begins to unfold at a point very near to the conclusion (after Pierre and Claire had already fallen in love with each other, and the future of the couple Pierre-Maria hung only on the thinnest of threads), because of the pounding repetition of certain very short lines ("It was 10:30. It was summer. Rodrigo Paestra."), because of the dialogue's sobriety and the impersonal descriptive interventions of the author. The suspenseful outer events of the deluge, the murders, and the suicide blend harmoniously with the explosive but unspoken inner events of the physical attraction between Pierre and Claire and the choking feeling of impotence that wells inside Maria.

Gérard d'Houville speaks of the added effect of the slow-motion cinematographic technique,[39] especially favored by the heroine's long night of vigil when, obliged to watch the closeness of the body of husband and rival sleeping on the floor of the overcrowded hotel corridor, and haunted by the specter of the fugitive whose nearness is not difficult to guess, she finally

makes the heroic effort of saving Rodrigo Paestra and of giving
a momentary significance to her own inimical fate. Her motions
to Paestra, the nocturnal drive along the deserted highway, their
silence, and her return to the hotel are so many brakes applied
to the irrepressible movement of time. The resulting *stillness*
gives a pathetic quality to the narrative. Moreover, this quality is
enhanced by an abundance of poetized passages, such as the
one in which Maria gives an unexpected aim to the clouds' electrical discharges: "The flashes of lightning kept lighting up the
shape of their [that of Pierre and Claire] desire"; or the one
in which she looks at Rodrigo Paestra while driving him to a
hiding place out of town: "Maria devoured him with her eyes,
devoured with her eyes this living prodigy, this black flower
which had bloomed that night in the licentiousness of love"; or
the description of her apprehension of the storm, that of thunder
and rain and that of the growing, magnetic sexual desire of the
others: "Maria didn't yet know the irresistible perfume of her
fear until then"; or, again, the relation of the heroine's ability
to sense poignantly and physically the infidelity of her husband
and the decaying aroma of the end of their marriage: "There
was about him the irreplaceable perfume of his power over her,
of his breach of love, of his wishing her well, there was about
her the odor of their dying love." Such passages lend the story
an appeal not frequently encountered in the totally decomposed
universe of Ionesco and Beckett, or in the mechanically rigid
world of other anti-novelists such as Alain Robbe-Grillet. The
short-lived infatuation with life of Marguerite Duras' characters glows with a catharsis that lingers, for the reader, long
after hero and heroine, fatigued, resigned, and humble, abort
and give up.

VIII L'Après-midi de Monsieur Andesmas

Thematically, the writer's tenth fiction publication is built
around the solitary waiting of the old man whose name appears
in the title. The novel is preceded by an epigraph called "Words
Overheard During the Summer of 1960," but the impatient
reader who hopes to find in it more than a vague clue to the
story can only be disappointed by its unrevealing text:

I have just bought a house. A very beautiful spot. Almost like Greece.
The trees around the house belong to me. One of them is enormous
and, in summer, will give so much shade that I'll never suffer from
the heat. I am going to build a terrace. From that terrace, at night,
you'll be able to see the lights of G. . . . There are moments here
when the light is absolute, accentuating everything, and at the same
time precise, relentlessly shining on one object. . . .

Actually, we soon learn, the heat is as intense as in other Duras
novels, and Monsieur Andesmas never gets to have his terrace
built during the course of the narrative.

The theme of waiting, explored by the author on numerous
other occasions, is here the very crux of the story. As in *Les
Chantiers*, little if anything else happens. A fatigued, obese old
man simply sits in front of his house located on a hilltop above
an unnamed Mediterranean village. As the book unfolds, a progressive lassitude, physical and spiritual, grips the hero and
causes in him an almost total disassociation from life. His waiting is practically uninterrupted, absolute; it is a profession, a
way of life as in the case of Jean of *Les Petits Chevaux de
Tarquinia*, as in the case of many other Duras characters. His
interest in others, in the noise and masks of the world, has already
diminished considerably through the years; and his old-man
reveries are tinged by passion only when he thinks of his
daughter, Valérie, absent throughout the course of the novel.
He had bought the house for her, had had it furnished according
to her wishes, and it is because of her that he is now waiting
for an architect, Michel Arc, to submit plans for the construction
of a terrace.

From time to time, the old man casts a glance on the village
below. There some sort of holiday is being celebrated. And the
gay musical fragments which sporadically reach his ears emphasize his painful loneliness and contrast, in mood and tempo, with
the static, petrified existence he leads. Yet, there is a definite
feeling derived from the narrative that Monsieur Andesmas does
not suffer nearly so much as perhaps does the reader who identifies himself with the hero. For the latter is already too *dis-
engaged* to experience fully the poignancy of the human condition which invariably encompasses solitude and waiting. As
a matter of fact, he becomes so used to loneliness and silence,

so comfortable that, when occasions for togetherness and conversation present themselves, he is increasingly reluctant to act:
"Mr. Andesmas' waiting began again. Oddly enough it was at
first calmer, more patient than a moment before. . . . Mr. Andesmas, who had claimed he could not bear waiting this way for
such a long time, is becoming more and more adjusted to the
wait. . . . Panick-stricken at again having to break so much silence,
Mr. Andesmas hunted for words." On the contrary, the reader
is *engaged* at least to the extent that he is interested in another's
plight, which might not be his initially but which become his as
he pursues the story's relentless focus on the irrepressible stagnation of the central character. His involvement, coupled with
and enhanced by the process of identification, appears to make
the reader more actively a part of that world, shortchanged and
defrauded, that the anti-novelist consistently disparages.

As we turn the pages of the novel we become aware of the
similarities and differences between Monsieur Andesmas and
the hero of *Les Chantiers*. Like him, Monsieur Andesmas cher-
ishes his solitude and makes little effort to cast it aside. Because
he is older, he experiences not only an intellectual delight in
loneliness but also an understandable feeling of repose, of quiet
ease and dignity of bearing. Whereas he methodic cultivation
of waiting resulted in insomnia for the protagonist of *Les Chantiers*, Monsieur Andesmas is quite able to fall asleep, periodically, in the chaise longue in which he waits, as he had waited
and slept, it seems, for as long as he could remember.

Having reached the age when death is no longer a remote
possibility, the laughter and the music from the village below
mingle, for Monsieur Andesmas, into a most ironic twist. Unlike the cry of the victim which, in *Moderato cantabile*, had
signaled for Anne Desbaresdes the feasibility of another existence, the possibility of real life, the merrymaking reaching Monsieur Andesmas' ears is an insult added to the incurable injury
of old age, with its decay of physical and mental capacities.
The story's leitmotif is a ludicrous pun on the hero's inability to
hope, to cling on to life:

> When the lilac blooms my love
> When the lilac blooms forever,

When our hope is here every day
When our hope is here forever

This inability is especially obvious in his attitude and thoughts on the occasion of the three visits paid to him during the course of the afternoon.

The first is that of a non-human, a dog. The animal emerges slowly from one of the paths of the slope, and when Monsieur Andesmas finally becomes aware of the presence he notices that it too "was staring at the same bright empty space [and was] panting from fatigue and from the heat." The sight of another being does not move the hero and he "does not show any sign of hostility or friendliness toward the dog." But his failure to react is not surprising to Monsieur Andesmas or to reader. As a matter of fact, there is little reason for reaction. He is waiting for a man, Michel Arc, not a dog; and besides, he has passed the age when it is physically possible for him to exhibit interest or emotion at the slightest opportunity. Finally, though, and only after the greatest effort, "the man gives him a friendly greeting." But it is too late, of course, for the dog has already started to retreat. Yet, the animal's disappearance is not followed by regret on the part of Monsieur Andesmas. There is still the sky and the mountain and the static air, still those lifeless surroundings hardly animated by the remoteness of life in the village below, still the waiting, the drowsiness of light sleep, the living coma of acute stillness in which he can sink, almost empty of desire, almost at peace.

The second visit is that of a subhuman, a retarded little girl, the architect's daughter who comes to inform the old man that her father is being detained in the village because of the festivities; he will be late. Monsieur Andesmas hesitates and does not find much to say beyond thanking her for letting him know about Michael Arc's reason for the delay. But the little girl remains, persists, and keeps staring stupidly at him. The hero then makes a feeble effort; mechanically, he takes a coin out of his pocket and hands it to the visitor. It is a useless gesture, surely more intended to pay her for her trouble and make her leave than to incite a conversation and prompt her to stay. But Monsieur Andesmas' expectations are not fulfilled. The girl asks if he has a message for her father. He is taken by surprise and does not find a suitable answer. The child, confused, puzzled, and clumsy, mumbles a few words, then drops and loses her coin. She would like to leave now, but, as in the case of the first visitor, Monsieur Andesmas believes it de rigueur to attempt to delay her disappearance. The tone and the words chosen are not convincing, however: "O, I have plenty of time, plenty of time, why don't you rest . . . take your time, take all the time you want, why don't you rest?" Awkwardly, wishing perhaps to persuade himself (more than the girl) that he is still capable of human relationships, of communication, that he is not capitulating without at least the semblance of a struggle, he makes, again, a futile, mechanical exertion which aborts in embryo.

The author informs us in the end: "Monsieur Andesmas tried to find something to say . . . but finding nothing, he remained silent." And as the child disappears down the mountain path, without regret, comforted by the thought of being alone once more, he watches her descend until he can see nothing of her, "nothing, not one speck of her blue dress," and he is again in that "state of abandonment whose disconcerting vastness she had only emphasized through her appearance." It should be noted, however, that the adjective "disconcerting" applies more to the feeling of solitude than contaminates the reader who has not lost all hope, who is younger, less incapacitated and more alive, than to the reaction of the hero who, according to John K. Simon, "takes refuge in an inner detachment" and whose "gradual absorption into the realm of subjectivity"[40] is a fait accompli.

The third and final visit is that of a mother of five children, the abandoned wife of Michel Arc. There is an obvious progression from the appearance of the dog, to that of the subhuman and the intensely human presence of a sensitive person who comes to tell Monsieur Andesmas that her husband will be very late because he is too busy down below, dancing and flirting with Valérie. The hero's initial reaction is to be found in a passage already quoted above: "Panick-stricken at again having to break so much silence, Monsieur Andesmas hunted for words." From that point on, however, there is, in the beginning, a progression also on the part of the protagonist's willingness to play a part in the difficult process of communication: almost entirely reluctant in the case of the dog, perhaps a little less hesitant when the little girl got ready to leave, he is now momentarily able to establish a vague contact with the architect's wife.

There is no dialogue, to be sure, for each pursues a conversation in monologue. The woman, in broken, awkward sentences, replete with innuendos and suggestive interpolations, tells the old man how it was she who had first noticed Valérie, her sparkling youth, her ineffable blondeness, and how she had thought that her long hair was perfect for a man to drown in, her own man—why not—to whom, strangely, she had introduced the little flirt. And Monsiuer Andesmas tells the woman about his love for his daughter, about the pleasant discovery he had made during the afternoon, between the visits and the periods of sleep, a discovery "which he had not had the time to make in the course of his life, and which, probably because of his age, tired him more than it should have, but which he felt was nevertheless a common one [and which] for convenience and perhaps also because of his failing vocabulary, he called the understanding of his love for his child." There is little consolation in all this for Michel Arc's wife. But she is not very demanding. She simply requires a perception, the suggestion of a nearness, not an actual shoulder to cry on but an assurance at least, that her words and her laments are not launched into the empty face of universal doom, but that they might, perhaps, fly by the ears of another human being and cause in him a reaction, a response, no matter how vague. For this might contradict the absoluteness of her solitude, that dreadful feeling of complete abandonment. That is why she had left the village behind, with its music and its dance and its noise, and she had climbed all the way up the mountain in search of someone, a relationship, another's eyes and ears and words. And Marguerite Duras comments: "Perhaps the conversation could go on like this, on the basis of the children, of this of her life as a mother [and his as a father]; perhaps it could move in this way, cheatingly, along the byways of the present hour." Cheatingly, of course, because her children are down below, taking part in the general celebration, unaware of the drama in their family; because Valérie, likewise, sings and dances, ignorant of the tragedy she is causing, a painful, inescapable presence to Madame Arc, a terrible absence to Monsieur Andesmas.

There is no action in this novel and, in the case of the hero, hardly an interior struggle. It is clear that his solitude will become irremediable, for the reader guesses that Valérie will run away with the architect. As in the case of Francou's mother, for him it is too late: he neither can nor will he act. As for Madame Arc, after her initial effort (limited to telling someone her story), she will accept suffering because she knows that she will one day forget. And resignation will perhaps be followed by another man, another marriage: "Some day," she opines without real hope but automatically and only as an outburst of the uncontrolled system of defense within her, "some day another man will come to me and under his eyes I will feel the signs of a first desire, that heaviness, that warmth in my blood, that I will surely recognize. The same thing will happen. No other man will be able to come close to me then, I won't be able to bear anyone, not even him, Michel Arc." In part, she uses the same words as those of the Maid in Le Square; but there is even less hope in her case and she is not capable of even the marginal enthusiasm her predecessor had exhibited. For unlike the protagonist of Le Square, she considers life to be neither absurd, nor unjust, but simply terribly mediocre. Sometimes we fall in love, we marry, we have children or a clandestine affair. Impossible passions and calamitous dramas occur, activity and change seem within reach, only to fade quickly and plunge the victims into the antechamber of hell where neither hope can animate nor desire can stop the onrush of permanent acquiescence.

L'Après-midi de Monsieur Andesmas ends, then, on a more pessimistic note than many of the previous novels. As the voices and the laughter of Michel Arc and Valérie are heard, closer and closer for they are now climbing up the mountain, the two characters continue to chat. Their clichés, however, do nothing but reveal their solitude. The uncaring, the happy couple returns to pick up Valérie's things, to say good-by. As they approach, there is one last, desperate attempt on the part of Madame Arc. Realizing that she has not really communicated to Monsieur Andesmas, that perhaps he has not understood what has happened, she pleads that he make an effort, to listen, to decipher through her feeble expressions his and her tragedy; this, not in order that he do anything about it but in order that there be a common ground between them, a consanguinity of drama and defeat. But the novel ends with the following three paragraphs:

"They'll be here in a few minutes," the woman implored. "I won't tell you anything more than what is necessary. I beg you."

"I won't listen to anything any more," Monsieur Andesmas warned her.

She spoke anyway, his hand on hers, in turn shaking it and stroking it, during the few minutes left before the dazzling appearance of the others, in front of the chasm filled with an evenly shaded light.

And it is obvious that the woman's words are just as futile as are the automatic gestures of the old man who strokes her hand as he might the back of a dog, without real sensitivity, untouched, robot-like.

Like *Le Square* and *Dix heures et demie du soir en été. L'Après-midi de Monsieur Andesmas* is precisely fixed in time. The hero's afternoon is short, lasting no longer than two hours, between four and six on a hot Saturday in the middle of summer. The brevity of the novel points to the fact that it takes little time for a man to effect that disassociation from life which is the subject of the story; it also demonstrates once more Marguerite Duras' ability to begin the unfolding of her plot at a point very near the end, in the best classical tradition. Aside from the engaging interest of the contents as a whole, the latter are not, however, the only qualities worth mentioning. Poetic-pathetic phrases and at times paragraphs dot the narration and increase its effectiveness. The following, describing part of Monsieur Andesmas' reaction to the disappearance of Michel Arc's daughter, is only one example of the many which could be given: "The echo of the childish voice floats for a long time, insoluble, around Monsieur Andesmas, then, none of its possible meanings having been retained, it moves off, fades, joins the various shimmerings, thousands of them, hanging in the chasm of light, becomes one of them. It disappears. Again Monsieur Andesmas finds himself alone. Alone waiting for a man without a sense of time. In the forest." John K. Simon finds, in addition, that "the Duras tone is occasionally self-parodied in stylistic affectations

(coyly inverted syntax, sighing repetitions, deliberately trouble-
some antecedents for pronouns),"[41] but the reviewer fails to
mention that these fit perfectly within the context: Monsieur
Andesmas' life is a parody; his failing intelligence cannot suggest thoughts formulated in correct syntax or morphology; and
repetitions of vocabulary serve to reveal the unchanging monotony of the hero's interior and exterior existence. In this connection, the commentary of Jacques Guicharnaud is one of the most
profound that critics have made, to date, on the writer's style.
"Madame Duras," he wrote, "makes mistakes in spelling and mistakes in grammar. She seems to have a vague idea about the
use of the subjunctive and the agreement of participles (French
editors respect the original text, even to spelling mistakes. One
never knows: the writer may have had a reason for them), but
she never makes a mistake in style, at least within the style
she has chosen."[42]

I Le Ravissement de Lol V. Stein

There is very little to please the reviewer in Madame Duras'
1964 fiction publication. Although there is no connection between Le Ravissement de Lol V. Stein and Les Impudents, not
since her debut in literature did she write a less effective novel.
In spite of the author's established reputation by this time and in
spite of the usual critical acclaim bestowed upon her works,
Marguerite Duras saw her cryptic story of a mentally deranged
woman greeted with sparing comment if not outright indifference. Robert André's opinion: "We read here, without doubt, the
most complex, the most subtle narrative (too subtle perhaps
because the word keeps popping ceaselessly into the reader's
mind) of Marguerite Duras,"[43] is about as complimentary as the
French critics have deigned to be on this novel. Anglo-Saxon
reviewers, perhaps more reminiscent of Freud and of Proust via
the often hallucinatory works of Faulkner and Julien Green, have
had slightly kinder words to say about Le Ravissement de Lol
V. Stein. Kenneth S. White stated at the end of his very short
review of the book: "While the narrative's substance is slim,
compelling overtones of characterization and the mysteriously
changing ebb and flow of a woman's despair distinguish this
memorable novel."[44] Stanley Kauffmann, after observing, not in

an unmocking tone, that the book "might have been written by a lady who had read Proust and Freud long ago and who had kept up with the vein of tacit, feminine sensibility that runs through much of the 20th-century fiction," notes in what appears to be an admiring comment that, "fundamentally, it is the author who hovers over the story, turning it this way and that to catch and lose light, to mock slightly the novelistically expected, to dramatize the pressure of modern ultra-consciousness both on the characters in the story and the author who is telling it."[45]

The teller, whose name (we learn it almost midpoint through the novel) is Jack Hold, a friend of the couple Tatiana and Peter Beugner and lover of Peter's wife, becomes aware of the presence of Lol Stein from the window of a hotel room where he meets his mistress. Lol delights in spying on the lovers from the rye field in which she lies, and this vicarious experience seems to compensate for the humdrum existence she leads next to a husband she had married on the rebound, following the shattering episode years ago when, about to become the wife of the man she loved, she was jilted and abandoned by him. Somehow her mind seemed to go along with Michael Richardson, the young man of her dreams, and she never quite recuperated from the nervous breakdown that ensued. Tatiana, witness of the drama, had apparently informed Jack Hold of some of the pertinent facts. But he does not know everything; and when he runs out of details, he imagines them (not unlike Chauvin of *Moderato cantabile*). The narrative is dotted with such phrases as: "This is what I surmise"; or "Here is my opinion"; or "This I invent, I see"; or "I'm convinced of absolutely nothing." There are, moreover, numberless question marks throughout the teller's remarks. This lack of precision is, of course, in keeping with the tenets of the New School, as is the alternation of present episodes with flashbacks and visions of the future often superimposed on one another, cross-fading and dissolving as on the cinema screen.

The relationship between Tatiana, Lol, and Jack Hold is obviously too complicated to admit a clear elucidation. Why does Tatiana tell her lover about her friend? What attracts him in a woman who is not particularly beautiful, who is at least partly demented, and who threatens to break his liaison with a mistress who, he agrees, gives him immeasurable physical satisfaction?

And why does Lol, the mother of three children and a faithful wife for a period of over ten years give herself to Jack Hold? Is it because he resembles Michael Richardson or because he reminds her of him? Perhaps, but the author has the heroine contradict the possibility which, although logical, need not have a place in a novel belonging to the New School. The only thing that is plain is that, for Lol to exist, it is necessary that Jack Hold think of her; and in order that he think of Lol, it is necessary that Tatiana furnish a number of details. Beyond that, the kaleidoscope of shifing prisms through which the (un)action moves is much like that of the film of Alain Robbe-Grillet, *Last Year at Marienbad*: consciously tricky, cryptically abstract, repetitious, and linguistically poetic.

Actually, Marguerite Duras' ability to maneuver words into catching, touching combinations ranging from sentence to paragraph length is the only pleasing quality of this novel. The following, describing a luncheon scene between Jack Hold and the heroine, points at once to the reiterating theme of consent in the writer's work and to the intriguing style of which she is so often capable: "We are eating. Another series of events might have taken place, other revolutions between people other than ourselves, with other names, other spans of inner time might have occurred, longer or shorter, other tales of oblivion, of a vertical descent into the oblivion of memory, of lightning-like access to other memories, of other long nights, of love without end, of God knows what? Lol is right. That does not interest me." The plot, dealing as it does with a demented person, contains many passages pointing to the slow decay of a human's spiritual life and to the vain efforts often made to postpone the inevitable paralysis of intelligence: "She was bored, so bored she wanted to scream. . . . The only time she did speak was to say how impossible it was for her to express how boring and long it was, to be Lol Stein. . . . The difficulty she experienced in searching for a single word seemed insurmountable. . . . Thoughts born and reborn, daily, always the same thoughts that came crowding in, come to life and breathe, in an accessible, boundless Universe, out of which one thought, and only one, eventually manages at long last to make itself heard, become visible, slightly more visible than the others. . . . I am beginning to understand, by slow degrees, inchingly slow. I see walls, smooth, offering nothing to grasp, they were not there a short while before, they have just risen around us." The occasional awkwardness of such passages in translation notwithstanding, the language remains moving, pounding, poetic.

But the tuned reader understands faster than the narrator, and no walls rise between his anticipation of the novel's end and the actual final events. As we have guessed, watching Tatiana make love to Jack Hold affords only an indirect and temporary pleasure to the bored, psychic, lifeless Lol. More is necessary: becoming acquainted with the narrator and moving on a more intimate plane with him are, of course, meaningful gestures toward change, toward incarnation. "We're moving toward something," she says to him at one point. "Even if nothing happens, we're moving toward some goal." But to his demand for specificity, as predictable, the only possible reply is: "I don't know. The only thing I know anything about is the immobility of life." And after in fact she has given herself to him and she has spent a few moments of mad rapture, there is nothing else to do but for Jack Hold to resume his deeper, more satisfying relationship with Tatiana, and for Lol to luxuriate once more in the vicarious, dubious delectation of watching them make love from the rye field in which she hides, underneath the window of the familiar hotel.

Le Ravissement de Lol V. Stein is, then, replete with themes and preoccupations we have encountered in most of the previous novels of Marguerite Duras. But the psychological framework in which they are clad, enhanced as it is by the heroine's mental illness, appears to constitute a return to the novel of analysis of the phenomena of consciousness, already overworked and played out before World War II. Marguerite Duras seems to have ignored, in this instance, Natalie Sarraute's ironic admonition that no French novelist can, as of the 1950s, pronounce the word "psychology" without blushing or feeling a sense of guilt.[46] In *Le Ravissement de Lol V. Stein* familiar patterns of human behavior emerge too rapidly and they become fundamental and compelling only through the analytical examination of the narrator, subtle, vague, painful, and uncertain as it may be. Direct

reader involvement is lacking, and the effectiveness of the novel
is thereby diminished.

X Le Vice-Consul

The last fictional publication to be considered in this study
is a gripping composition of a semiplotless story that comes very
close to matching most of the characteristics of the New School.
Since the appearance of *Le Vice-Consul* in 1966, Marguerite
Duras has not written any other original novel, although the
play *Les Viaducs de la Seine-et-Oise* has come out in fictional
form in 1968 under the title *L'Amante anglaise*. Articles, essays,
and plays continue to be penned by her at an almost incessant
pace, but it is doubtful that the author has exhausted her "taste"
for novel-writing. Be this as it may, *Le Vice-Consul* is worthy
of attention not only because of its inherent literary value but
also because it is, to date, the last original narrative of the writer.

The plot, whatever there is of it, is dual: on the one hand,
there is the haunting story of an Oriental girl, chased away by
her mother because of a youthful mistake that resulted in pregnancy; on the other, there is the description of the cosmopolitan
world centering around the French Embassy in Calcutta, a world
of partying political functionaries in which Peter Morgan, the
author of the story mentioned, moves. Throughout the novel,
the two worlds, that of the physically dispossessed (the poor,
the starving, and the leper) and that of the spiritually deprived
(the bored, the alcoholic, and the semilunatic), are constantly
juxtaposed in such a way as to achieve "a somewhat hypnotic
effect upon the reader."[47] This effect is arrived at by the use of
standard anti-novel devices: unfinished sentences, subconversations, hidden allusions, innuendos, shady paragraph structure,
repetitions, mysterious and unexplained situations, and, at times,
a highly poetic utilization of language.

Jean-Marc de H., Vice-Consul at Lahore, has been removed
from his post because, without any apparent reason, he has shot
a gun into the Shalimar Gardens, a depository of lepers and dogs.
His shots were not aimed at anyone in particular, but some
(lepers, or dogs, or both) died as a result of the accident. While
French officials study the case, he is sent to Calcutta, site of the
Embassy. Here he becomes involved with the drinking crowd
of the diplomatic corps and befriends the Ambassador's wife,

Anne-Marie Stretter. The latter, beautiful but no longer young, appears to be the only character really alive in the book. She attracts around her the playboys of the different nations having diplomatic relations with India, and she seems to provoke a certain amount of confabulation at the soirées she gives, to lend a certain air of substance to the flimsy guests, to hold them together as satellites circling around her affable and charming personality. Perhaps she will become interested in the deposed Vice-Consul, perhaps she will admit him in the not-so-restrained group of lovers she already has. But although they dance, drink and converse (as personages in anti-novels do), the author is careful not to clarify anything and to force the reader-accomplice to weave, on his own, the many dangling strands of the plot. All we learn at the end of the novel is that Jean-Marc de H. will, probably, be sent to Bombay and, probably, the whole unintelligible affair will be forgotten by everyone concerned.

The narrative's cryptic allusions and failure to pursue to some logical end the promised beginnings (the story of the pregnant girl; the mystery surrounding the shooting incident) are given an impatient and unfriendly look by two constant detractors of the New School in general and of Marguerite Duras in particular: Kléber Haedens and André Thérive. The first, after criticizing the fact that much effort is needed to go through *Le Vice-Consul*, takes the author to task for her handling of the Cambodian girl's story: "The obvious purpose of these chapters about the wretched girl is to remind us that Marguerite Duras keeps her attention firmly fixed on the black side of the world's misery. There is, however, something far too mechanical about this compulsory compassion for us to be greatly affected by it; all the more so in that the story of the unhappy Cambodian girl is not, so to speak, true [it is part of the novel by Peter Morgan]. . . . Consequently the most realistic parts of the book end up by losing their realism."[48] A novel about a novel is not anything new in twentieth-century French literature,[49] and besides, no realism is actually lost since the very first sentence of the book informs us that Peter Morgan is an author about to write a story. Bettina L. Knapp's comment on this part of *Le Vice-Consul* is not only more complimentary but also more just and correct: "The most striking of the many impressionistic portraits drawn by Marguerite Duras is that of a seventeen-year-old girl, homeless, destitute, groveling, mixing with lepers, screeching in her half-dazed state of madness as she struggles to survive in this steaming and crushing world."[50] The seeker of *real* reality can, of course, go back to the powerful *Un Barrage contre le Pacifique* and other early novels of Marguerite Duras, but he need not conclude, as Kléber Haedens does, that *Le Vice-Consul* "is pure Durasian mishmash," and that "the truth is that Mme. Duras can't write."[51] Such a conclusion is worthy of note only because it represents the hurried, outmoded dismissal of conservative critics of compositions and of styles which portray the deeper, more penetrating reality of our world made up at least in part of mishmash, of stammerings, of unfinished and unexplainable actions. The second reviewer, André Thérive, decries likewise what he calls the "suicide" of literature of which the antinovelists are allegedly guilty. According to him this suicide is due to the snobism of the avant-garde. And he explains: "What is this snobism? The mania to show reality as irrational."[52] What the critic appears unwilling or unable to accept—no doubt because such an acceptance would be difficult and because it would cast suspicion on modes that are comfortable to live with, if not altogether consoling—is that there is a great deal of irrationality in life, and that it is the task of writers to confront us with it and thereby impart to us a measure of their own precious lucidity. As to his contention, not unlike that of Kléber Haedens, that Marguerite Duras' style resembles, "in large part, a hidden inability, a great difficulty to conceive and to express,"[53] the novelist's works and their general popularity contradict the conservative's untenable position. To equate a hero's inability to conceive and express with the author's is to forget that one of the prime aims of the New School is precisely that of shocking us into thinking and into communicating our thoughts by means of a frank confrontation with the difficulties usually connected with such processes. The strange harshness of André Thérive's review of *Le Vice-Consul* would have been diminished, perhaps, had he paid a closer attention to the text (he spells the heroine's name as Streller instead of Stretter), had he made the effort required, without which (as Kléber Haedens had observed but should not have deplored) it is impossible to render justice to any anti-novelist.

Actually, the many themes explored by Marguerite Duras in

previous publications, ranging from interest in social problems to concern with the impossibility of communication, from desire for change to effort toward amelioration and final consent of the status quo, are masterfully alluded to in this novel, in the broken sentences and in the quasi-filmed, circle-turning movements of the personages. Noteworthy as an example of superior writing in *Le Vice-Consul* is the fact that now, no longer wishing to preach as she had done in *Un Barrage contre le Pacifique*, the spectacle of extreme poverty next to riches and waste prompts the author to much more effective, cold-blooded descriptions of the anomalies of justice. In a half-page chapter following several which related a soirée at the Embassy, Marguerite Duras resumes briefly and in staccato manner the progress of the Cambodian girl's march, now interrupted by the bright lights and the odor of food emanating from the luxurious edifice: "Under the lamppost, scratching her bald head, she, thinness of Calcutta on this night so fat, she is seated among the lunatics, she is there, void of ideas, her heart dead, still waiting for some food. . . . Much food is being ejected tonight from the kitchens of the French Embassy. . . . She eats with fantastic speed, she avoids the crowds of other madmen, their blows; her mouth full, she laughs until she becomes breathless." What a difference, also, between previous descriptions of dying children, moving but long and labored, and the tight, sober writing relating the death scene of the girl's child: "The baby does not drink. The milk flows on him, but does not go in. What remains of life [in the child] serves only to refuse to live. . . . The belly of the child is a balloon full of air and of worms." Moreover, the vain efforts of the characters to communicate, their stutterings, their perseverance, through trial and error, their capitulation, are rendered more poignantly than in any preceding novel in the senseless dialogue of the men and women who attend the soirée at the Embassy: for their questions about and to the Vice-Consul remain totally unanswered; no one is capable of solving the riddle, neither the guests, nor the officials who have seen his dossier, nor the hero himself. "Can you tell us anything more, anything at all?" he is being constantly asked. And when the futility of physicial and intellectual exertion can no longer be eluded, he concludes: "I have the impression that if I tried to tell you what I should like to be able to say, everything would crumble into dust . . . the words to tell you, you, the words . . . about me . . . to tell you, they don't exist. I would make errors, I would use those . . . to tell you something else . . . something that happened to another . . ."

But the mystery of the story need not be solved, and the characters need not come out of real or imagined impasses: for the fact is that "the reader is perpetually engrossed and swept along in the ominous progression of this tale, like a pebble caught in an avalanche."[54]

XI Summary

The seven titles discussed under the present heading reveal, then, an author adhering progressively more and more to the anti-novel vein. Her association with the movement must not be interpreted, however, as a blind attachment to it. With the few exceptions noted (in *Les Chantiers* for example, in *L'Après-midi de Monsieur Andesmas*), Marguerite Duras has been able to adapt and modify the characteristics of the New School[55] in order to suit better her own artistic makeup and in order not to fall into the trap of the totally dehumanized creations of some of her colleagues. For with lesser or greater difficulty her stories can be summarized, her personages remain identifiable and recognizable human beings, and vague but viable hope illuminates, in part, the situations in which she places heroes and heroines. The pessimism of some of the works notwithstanding, utopian incarnation manages to make the characters come out, temporarily, from their acute isolation; and then simulation of conversation is possible, human vulnerability becomes tolerable, and the personages are able to catch a furtive glimpse of the joy of living before the disaster of defeat takes over and conquers permanently. Marguerite Duras is not just another member of the New School, preoccupied solely with the emptiness of human existence and with the complete absurdity of all life. More susceptible to human bonds, to the possibility of hope, to the pain and pleasure to be derived from human emotions, her involvement with the anti-novel is personal and special, and there is, then, little wonder that it has helped to intensify so much the limelight cast upon her ever since the publication of *La Vie tranquille*.

CHAPTER 5

The Plays

I *French Theater Since World War II*

IN terms of percentage, probably no other country can boast of so many theatergoers as France. Government-sponsored and enthusiastically supported by the public, theatrical groups prosper in the capital and outside of it. It is no exaggeration to say that, all things being equal, the French intellectual would rather see a play than view a movie, go to the opera, or listen to a concert. The reasons for this are both too obvious and too varied for elucidation. Suffice it to point out that, in the country of Molière, the theatrical tradition is so well entrenched, has flourished so persistently throughout the centuries, and has renewed itself so boldly that no contemporary competitor—neither the cinema, nor television, nor the automobile and the weekend exodus—could diminish public interest or box-office receipts.

Since World War II great contributions to the French theater have been made not only by authors but even more particularly by imaginative stage directors such as Jean-Louis Barrault, Roger Blin, André Reybaz, and Georges Vitaly, to mention only a few. These artists have displayed a revolutionary audacity in stripping dramatic productions of traditions dating back to the seventeenth century, and in adopting instead the practices of the "total theater"[1] according to which the spectator must be made to face, directly and without explanation, the conflict on the stage, without the *benefits* of story, of exposition, of psychological or social or any other form of analysis.

Jean Vilar's *Théâtre National Populaire* became an established institution, responding to the most varied public taste with the most diverse performances: these often ranged from plays by Pierre Corneille to those of Heinrich von Kleist, from dramas

117

by Bertold Brecht to the poetic dramatizations of Henri Pichette.[2] The more recent popularity of the anti-theater,[3] corresponding on the stage with the movement of the anti-novel, has provided a revitalized and intriguing public interest in the odd activities and apparent meanderings but really meaning-charged clichés of lonely, bored, and extremely depressed personages. Devoid of tradition, conformity, and open to all myths, the anti-theater has discovered new vistas and has recaptured that ancient form of tragedy that one found in the Greek theater and in the *Mystères* of the Middle Ages. Its total freedom has appealed to most contemporary literary giants who, although in the main novelists or essayists, have all tried their hand at the writing of engaging and absorbing plays. Among the female writers who have made important strides are Françoise Sagan, Simone de Beauvoir, Nathalie Sarraute and Marguerite Duras.

Madame Duras came to the theater, understandably enough, because of her constant ability to pack complexities into the banalities of daily dialogue. Her passage from the novel to drama was not a difficult one. Already in her stories she had been able to avoid long descriptions and to rely mainly on conversation for the development and the diffusion of conflicts. It was an apparently easy task to pursue the process of sobriety in writing to the more demanding style of dramatic composition.

II   Les Viaducs de la Seine-et-Oise

Madame Duras' first play is based on the newspapers' account of an apparently senseless murder committed by a pair of sexagenarians in the department of Seine-et-Oise. The event took place in 1954 when parts of a human body were discovered in a number of train cars arriving in different stations throughout France. Anthropological research showed that the parts, put together, constituted the body of a woman. The state-owned Railway Company, S.N.C.F., conducted its own investigation and came up with the curious fact that, no matter what the final destination of the train cars was, on the way, they had all passed over the viaduct of Epinay-sur-Orge. The police managed to arrest the murderers, an elderly man and his wife, a peaceful couple of retired employees of the S.N.C.F. They discovered further that the victim was their crippled cousin, who had lived in their home for some twenty-seven years. Apparently, there had been no friction between the three. At any rate, neither the police nor the court could establish any motive, nor could the guilty advance any. The case remained, therefore, a mystery for the defenders of justice and for the killers as well. His condemnation to death and hers to life imprisonment terminated the public's involvement with all concerned.

These curt facts are carefully recalled to the audience before the rise of the curtain. *Les Viaducs de la Seine-et-Oise,* presented in 1960, is the author's only two-act play and her longest dramatic composition to date. Act I has only two personages, Claire and Marcel, the two sexagenarians. They talk about the murder they had committed, about the discovery of the different parts of the body, about their impending arrest. Throughout the monologue-interspersed dialogue there is a desperate search for the reasons which prompted the murder. In the play the victim is portrayed as the couple's cook, and Marcel especially misses the good dishes she used to prepare and serve. Marie-Thérèse Ragond was not only a good servant, but she also had the added advantages of being deaf and dumb, of living an inconspicuous existence (except for an occasional, nocturnal rape at the hands of Alphonso, a character who will appear in Act II) devoted entirely to her masters. Looking back, neither Claire nor Marcel can come up with acceptable motives for their crime. Perhaps they did it because they had looked forward to the long, painful, risky job of cutting up the body and getting rid of it. "It was a tough and new type of work," Marcel says at one point, ". . . a job that took so very long, to make all those pieces disappear. . . ." The key word here is the adjective *new.* It appears that the couple had always lived the uneventful, dull existence of public employees who have nothing but retirement to look forward to in their youth, and death to wait for after they no longer work. This is evident in the following bit of dialogue:

MARCEL: How anonymous we used to be. People in town talked about how famous we were in anonymity. They said the Ragonds as one would say (*he searches*) artichokes or the weather!
CLAIRE: I never heard anyone mention us anywhere. She on the other hand, of course, they spoke about her. Being deaf and dumb is rather unusual, people talked about her . . . but us? Less than of artichokes . . .

MARCEL: Yes, my Claire.
CLAIRE: Wouldn't that be why, after all, because she was among the living in town, even though she was deaf and dumb?

It seems that those who merely exist cannot tolerate those who are really alive because they constitute a proof of the former's lack of vitality.

The couple's lucidity is perhaps surprising, for one wonders how, were it not for the author's imposition of her own clairvoyance on the protagonists, simple people like Marcel and Claire could see so clearly the hidden significance of so terrible an act as the murder they had committed. Marcel especially appears to be able to look beyond the appearances, often to surmise correctly and sometime to point out how, far from giving in to the mediocrity of his destiny, he would react, occasionally, he would make a number of efforts, however minute, however futile: "I try," he says. "I make some efforts. A little bit of gymnastics every morning . . . a little walk in the afternoon when I go buy the newspaper . . . a little of this . . . a little of that . . . I try. . . " He it is, too, who attempts to impress upon his wife the necessity of springing back to life in some fashion, in ways other than violent: "I beg you, one last time, become astonished about something, once, only once. Come back to me, my love, one last time." But for her it is too late. She no longer has the capacity of becoming involved, of attempting to change her lot, of making plans. The best she can do is to live in the past. Once she had been taken to the opera and she had heard *La Traviata*. The overture of Verdi's work haunts her throughout the play. It is all she has. "The memory of *La Traviata* pursues me . . . it makes me tear . . . melt in ecstasy." The stage directions specify that the melody is audible, repeatedly, and it is actually heard even at the end of the play when husband and wife are taken away by the police. Verdi's overture, which Claire cannot forget, contrasts pointedly with the awful crime she likewise is unable to banish from her memory. The two parallel recollections do not cancel each other: they are able to coexist, to give to her life a passable aura of acceptability.

And so it is that, unlike most personages of anti-plays, Claire and Marcel can await, without any notion of self-annihilation, the inevitable end. More than that, Marcel is even capable of loving life in spite of its miserable mediocrity. He not only exercises, walks, and reads his newspaper daily, but he also attempts to think of alibis he could use after his arrest, of the explanations he could offer. Although he is hungry, for example, he refuses to eat in the hope that thin criminals are pitied more than fat ones. And he adds: "They must not understand anything about it [the crime]. They should understand only one thing, that is that we don't understand anything about it ourselves. Let them be shocked by our good will. We should show a spirit of cooperation [in the vain search for motives] that would make even stones weep. (*Aside*) I think this is one detail that will save my life." And the conclusion of the defense should be: "Children, children, that's all these murderers are, members of the jury." When Claire points out to him that the strategy might not work, he still refuses to give up: "I shall defend myself nevertheless," he shouts. "I'll say everything. Her affair with Alphonso! Everything! . . . I persist in not wanting to be decapitated. (*Enthusiastically*) I shall say that she threatened us, I'll say anything . . . anything."

Marcel's optimism in the face of disorder, darkness, and death is even more obvious in the second act which takes place in Bill's café. Claire and her husband had gone there because there is nothing else to do while waiting to be arrested. The other customers, the Italian Alphonso and a mysterious Amoureux and Amoureuse (the first turns out to be a policeman), talk about the murder, the news of which has everyone in an uproar. The conversation, which first centers on the specific details reported by the newspapers, switches into a discussion on a topic that is at the very core of contemporary communication dilemmas. Samuel Beckett is perhaps the first to have pointed it out concisely: "There is nothing to express, nothing with which to express, nothing from which to express, no power to express, no desire to express, together with the obligation to express."[4] Marguerite Duras' vision of this dichotomy between impossibility and obligation contains a ray of hope which is absent from most antidramatists. The following passage exemplifies this view which we have already seen in her novels:

ALPHONSO: . . . But if one is sure that no one understands . . .
MARCEL: Yes, Mr. Alphonso, it is worth it. A chance in a thousand to be understood is worth the trouble of saying.
ALPHONSO: Why?
MARCEL: I do not know.

BILL: . . . Because there is no limitless desert anywhere, ever. One hopes, then, that what one says will take root some time, somewhere, even if it takes a thousand years, you understand Mr. Alphonso? . . .

ALPHONSO (*desperately and in a low voice*): It happens that one time in a thousand I understand, but when it happens, oh, what a joy!

During their wait, then, Claire and Marcel talked, with each other and with others, about what they had done, about the reasons for their act, about its consequences, and about the means of avoiding punishment. Their search for meaning, for sense in an alogical world, did not have entirely satisfactory results. But they did manage to perceive certain flashes, a number of dim lights flickering in the distance. For in spite of everything Marcel was able to look back, nostalgically, to gymnastics, walks, newspapers and, yes, to the intriguing job of a cadaver's dismemberment; and to look ahead, hopefully, to how he might exhort pity from jury and clemency from judge. And Claire too, with all her profound pessimism, was able to find a trace of support in Verdi's overture. Marcel will be executed, of course, and Claire will receive life imprisonment. But the "essential thing is not to regret anything, ever," Bill says in his penultimate speech, after the policeman identifies the murderers to him. The fact is that Claire and Marcel had acted, had moved against their destiny of placid, apathetic, forgotten pensioners of the S.N.C.F. At the point of a knife they had been able to communicate with the deaf and dumb Marie-Thérèse and to alert the impassive Universe of their own impassive existence. In terms of any standard morality their violence is inexcusable; in the midst of an absurd world in which the possibility of saying and doing becomes more and more questionable, any act carries with it a ready-made justification.

As in most of her recent novels, Marguerite Duras points also, in her first play, to the absolute necessity of never quite giving up, of never capitulating entirely. Man's dignity requires the effort more than the result, as in the case when the action contradicts laws and causes the death of the one who acted. Attempting to give meaning to one's meaningless existence is viewed by her as an eminently worthy deed; and the popularity of *Les Viaducs de la Seine-et-Oise* demonstrates that the public shares, although intuitively, the brilliant preoccupations of the author—as it proves, of course, that she is highly capable of capturing knotty, contemporary problems (the play is based, after all, on an actual case) and of reorchestrating them into lucid literary compositions that shed light on the terrible impasses we are forced to face in our terrestrial existence.

III Les Eaux et forêts

Marguerite Duras' second play was first published in *La Nouvelle Revue Française* in 1962. Three years later, on May 14, 1965, it was presented on the stage. During the course of the same year the drama was incorported in *Théâtre I.*

"Les Eaux et forêts" owes its title to the following passage in the play: "No, no, no . . . I must not listen, Mrs. Thompson; nothing; I must not pay attention to anything . . . Everyone should be as I am, belong to the Waters and Forests, without any prejudices whatsoever, to belong at the same time to the waters and the forests . . . to have a part in everything . . . in nothing . . . in nothing at all."

This cryptic speech is made by Man. He, Woman 1, and Woman 2 are the only three protagonists of the one-act piece. Man, at the rise of the curtain, has been bitten by a dog apparently belonging to Woman 1. They talk about the event. Man complains. Woman 1 proposes that they all take a taxi and go to the Institut Pasteur for help. Man refuses. Woman 1 and Woman 2 insist. Conversation and monologue succeed each other. Remarks and facts become blurry, to interlocutors and spectators. For example, who is Woman 1? Is she Mrs. Thompson, as Man calls her at one point? Or Mrs. Johnson, as he and Woman 2 address her at another? Or Mrs. Simpson, as she is called later in the play? Or Marguerite-Victoire Sénéchal, as Woman 2 seems to recollect toward the end? And how does Man know so much about her? How does he guess what she did in 1932, on the shores of the Lac des Settons? Is he the one she used to dance with, those haunting Argentine tangos he refers to? Woman 1 addresses him as Mr. Thompson, later in the play. Is he, was he her husband? Man appears to be young, but the beginning stage indications do not specify his age. Woman 1 believes, for her part, that her husband was at least one hundred years old. "And I had enough of him," she declares, "up to my neck, right up to my neck. For the most uninvolved type of week-end he needed six weeks of preparation. Shots, vitamins, six weeks, and I had enough, up to my neck, and I couldn't stand it any longer." When we learn that he died falling in the Rhine, we suspect that she pushed him; she actually confesses the murder in her final speech. Yet, Man seems as alive as the other two, unless, of course, the whole scene takes place in hell.

Be it as it may, Man, who at the beginning of the play concludes that he alone is human and that conversation with anyone else is impossible, continues to talk nevertheless, on a number of topics, ranging from dogs to big-city problems, from his personal riches, unexpectedly blown out of proportion (seven children, a good job at the Mazarine Library, a superb wife, a Mercedez-Benz which might, incidentally, be the wife he is talking about, first-class furniture, property, property, a great deal of free time, a park full of fruit trees, lots of grass, etc.) to the most obviously phony self-praise and aggrandizement: "And not only I have," he boasts "but I do, I do, I act, I'm on the go. I do. I think. I change. I do. I think. I change. Sometimes I think, I think (*quicker and quicker diction*), sometimes I think of what I do, sometimes I don't, I do what I think, I think, I do, I think, I think, I do. . . ." But a comma later he explodes: "I have enough of it, I have enough of it . . . enough." For, he explains, "sometimes I'm wrong. I want to think, I make mistakes, I'm confused, I don't know where I am, I'm full of despair." Little wonder when at the end of the play, like Woman 1, he confesses that he had lied, that he had no job at the Mazarine Library, that he had never amounted to anything at all. Reincarnation remains utopian, but for a moment he had looked great, he had managed to fool his interlocutors, even himself.

Woman 2, a minor character by comparison to the others, also has a momentary limelight cast upon her. Woman 1 had, perhaps still has a husband, a dog and her visits to the Institut Pasteur; Man had, perhaps still has a wife, a number of dreams and two avid listeners in the female personages of the play; Woman 2 is content with a secret. Her own husband, Duvivier, a vicious man who in his youth had abused her sexually, is now becoming impotent. She hints that the secret might concern an extramarital love affair. She talks freely about it, but will not divulge what it is—except in her final speech when she confesses that it is simply an absence, a void, that in fact there is no secret at all, there is only Duvivier.

Reincarnation is utopian, then, in the case of all three characters. But an attempt has been made to raise oneself above the unbearable empty existence one is condemned to. For a while one has talked, has invented, and has deluded others and oneself. Little does it matter that the truth finally comes out. There will be other occasions, other listeners, perhaps even the same ones, and the entire *game* can begin anew after a brief interlude: the stage directions at the end of the drama specify that Man begins to hum a song, and the two women proceed to tap their feet to the beat. The three do not separate, and it is likely that the conversation will reinaugurate itself. We recall Man's speech quoted above and containing the title of the play. His apparent desire to remain aloof, to be at the same time of the waters and the forests, to have a part in everything and in nothing, is not fulfilled. He needs Woman 1 and Woman 2 as listeners, to lean on, but also as interlocutors, to listen to, to compare their misery to his, and to seek catharsis in theirs. The author's constant concern for Man's solitude and his need of others reappears, then, poignantly, in the dramatic dialogue under discussion.

The theme of abortive metempsychosis as a momentarily efficient tool in combating the mediocrity of life is well supplemented in "Les Eaux et forêts" with the blatant appeal of frequent comic sallies. Man's vision of Paris in the grips of raging rabies immobilizing people and automobiles, with red and green lights alone functioning and directing unseen pedestrians, is only one example of the writer's mordant humor. On the other side of the coin, and acting as a detraction, is the persistent use of scatology, especially by Woman 1, for no other apparent reason than its questionable shocking effect. Her concern for the sexual mores of canines, her scrupulous count of the number of times a day her dog urinates, the description of how she eats in its company, on the floor, the very same food, lend a foul stench to what would otherwise be, perhaps, a more successful excursion, for Marguerite Duras, in the field of dramatic literature. As it is, "Les Eaux et forêts" does not seem to occupy a major place in the dramatist's work. While the play did have a modestly successful run in a small Parisian theater, it is not of the type that appeals to a large public. Its vulgarities tend to alienate the elite, and the cerebral quality of many of the lines is over the head of the uninitiated. Morevoer, the continuity of the action lags, as it does in so many anti-plays, because the dialogue is often interrupted by time-consuming, action-stopping subconversations. An American commentator remarked: "her plays are good to read but offer only small dramatic interest. One might call them short stories in the form of dialogue."[5] This curt judgment is essentially correct in regard to "Les Eaux et forêts"; however, referring as it does to all the plays in *Théâtre I*, it is, as we shall see, a most debatable and too general an appreciation.

IV *"La Musica"*

The last play of *Théâtre I* is not the product of the modified antidramatist we have seen her to be in *Les Viaducs de la Seine-et-Oise* and "Les Eaux et forêts. "La Musica," presented in 1965 on a double bill with "Les Eaux et forêts," is rather a traditional piece, a tender, moving one-act play that squarely poses before us the unsolvable problem of the relationship between Man and Woman. Immediately following the dramatic version of *Le Square*, "La Musica" treats of the post-marital part of this relationship. In *Le Square*, the novel and the play, the difficulties of communication between sexes had led to a suspended state: neither the maid nor the traveling salesman will pursue the chance meeting in a city park to a more stable, more enduring union. In "La Musica" the couple had met and married before the rise of the curtain; but it had also separated and divorced prior to appearance on the stage. Thus, in classical fashion, the story begins very near its end.

Anne-Marie Roche and Michel Nollet are the only two protagonists. Several other voices are heard from behind the stage, or at the other end of telephone conversations, but the speakers are not seen, and this adds, of course, to the touching simplicity of the action. Former husband and wife meet on the neutral but terribly anonymous ground of a hotel lobby, in a town which is familiar to them and to which they had both come for the final divorce proceedings. The theme of lovers' return to a

site that had witnessed better and happier days is a standard
Romantic topic of prose and poetry, amply treated in the pre
and post-Romantic periods of French and other literatures. It
is, because of the frequency with which we encounter it, a banal
theme, to be sure, but one of universal appeal nevertheless, because it is so easy to identify ourselves with the feelings that
usually arise from it. Spleen, nostalgia, both a reluctance and a
need to compare present with past, the surprise caused by
change, deterioration and old age, the realization that neither
things nor beings could resist the corrosion of time, all these
aspects of one's journey into the *good old days* are brought out
effectively in "La Musica." We learn, for example, that the town
has altered considerably and, as a final attack against the peace
and serenity the lovers had known there, even an airport is in the
process of being built. He and she talk about a house they used
to know, and we find out that: nothing seems changed, the living
room is as it was, each piece of furniture is in its place, even
the television, "but there are other people in it, not the ones the
house had been sold to originally, different people, whom they
do not know, strangers dining in silence, who made them feel so
uneasy . . . so uneasy."

This feeling of constraint is punctuated throughout the play
by the forced smiles and laughter of the two characters. As a
matter of fact, stage indications specifically instructing the actors
on this point dot the conversation continuously, and these,
added to numerous other directions, mar somewhat the reading of "La Musica." Viewing it, however, is another matter.
Anne-Marie and Michel capture easily the sympathy of spectators who have been or have dreaded being caught in a similar
situation. For what should the relationship between a divorced
man and woman be? Should it be inimical? Should it be based
on sincere friendship, on cool politeness, on indifference? Or
should the memory of sweeter moments become dominant and
cause a rebirth of fondness for one another, of love? Marguerite
Duras' personages seem to *fall* for the latter version—not immediately, of course— and it is precisely their gradual *fall* that gives
the play a pathetic, yet cathartic quality.

To begin with, the chance meeting between Anne-Marie
and Michel had actually come about because of a reciprocal
desire to meet: this is pointed out by Michel's present mistress

who remarks, in a telephone call she places to him, that the lawyers could have easily handled the final proceedings in their absence. Moreover, neither he nor she oppose more than a faint resistance to the idea of beginning a conversation that is going to last for several hours:

MICHEL: Why shouldn't we talk to each other?
ANNE-MARIE: Why should we?
MICHEL: Just like that . . . we have nothing else to do.

True as far as it goes, since they both must wait for transportation till morning, one suspects that the official separation which has just become effective provides, ironically enough, a springboard from which communication is much more feasible than it could ever be in the premarital or marital state. It is obvious that there is a certain amount of detachment now, a lack of restraint which makes sincerity less painful, a sad feeling, too, that there is nothing more to lose.

Husband and wife hesitate, of course, and they speak at first only because silence is often more embarrassing than an exchange of banalities; but soon clichés give way to confessions, and it becomes evident that the rapport between them is stronger now than in the past. For example, he no longer hesitates to tell her about the other woman; she has no compunction to talk about her marriage plans and about her projected departure for America. Yet, the past interests them much more than the future. Looking back, it is difficult to understand what had happened, how things had deteriorated to the point of divorce: "We were young," he says, "we were married with the consent of everyone . . . they were all content, your family, mine, everyone, yes . . . we had everything we needed, a house, furniture . . . you had your furcoat. . . ." The fruitless search for reasons brings back unbearable memories: "For a yes, for a no," she recalls, "we gave ourselves so many nights of insomnia, we made so many scenes . . . scenes . . . and dramas, and. . . ." Later, she confesses that she had attempted to commit suicide when he had asked for a divorce, but in retrospect, the aborted act appears vulgar and useless. He admits that once, in a fit of jealousy caused by her repeated adulteries, he had bought a revolver and had planned to kill her. "You knew," she remarks, "that in this sort of case acquittal is in order." He knew it, of course,

yet he had abandoned the plan and decided to throw the gun
into the sea. Even more important than these dramatic acknowl-
edgements is the couple's probe into the motives of adultery.
Apparently neither had ever committed it because of a senti-
mental atachment for another person. What then, causes people
in love to seek others, whom they do not love? For adultery is
always calculated, always willed. And the initial regrets are
soon erased by repetition, by habit, and one begins to enjoy it,
to depend on it, to be unable to do without. Is it because of such
a trivial reason as the fact that he did not dance and she liked
to? Is it because, without knowing it, they were falling out of
love? Or is it in order to find again those first moments, that
rapture that one can no longer duplicate in the arms of one's
spouse?

But none of these possibilities seems plausible. No single
deficiency in the other could prompt so serious a step as adultery.
After all, "you know, it's terrible to be unfaithful, for the first
time . . . it's simply awful," she opines, and it is surely not worth
doing for petty reasons. Moreover, both Anne-Marie and Michel
realize, at least intuitively, that the present attraction they feel
for each other precludes the possibility of their having fallen
out of love at an earlier date. And since their infidelities were
not caused by affection for the others, what guarantee was there
of recapturing that singular bliss they had known only in the
days of old? Perhaps, then, the only explanation is that provided
by Anne-Marie who, a bit spitefully, but above all clairvoyantly
and sadly confesses: "He was simply a man other than you. No
other reason, that's it, he was another. You were on one side,
alone, and on the other side there were all the men whom I
would never know. (Pause) I think you probably understand
this perfectly. (Pause) Don't you?" Michel's affirmative reply,
which follows without hesitation, would seem to indicate that
his former wife's interpretation is more reasonable than any of
those they had thought of before. Husbands' and wives' need
of the unknown is viewed, then, as being more powerful than
laws, vows, and reason itself. Au fond de l'inconnu pour trouver
du nouveau (in the depths of the unknown [i.e., hell or heaven]
in order to find something new) Baudelaire had summed up,[6]
and the couple's conclusion is no different than that of the poet.
Love, marriage, adultery, and divorce are simply steps in man's

uncontrolled learning and discovery processes, unavoidable steps in a society that is both governed by customs and unable to cope with them. The author appears to imply that the sexes' need for order and stability (love and marriage) cannot help being contradicted by a parallel and stronger hunger for mystery and freedom (adultery and divorce). And there is no solution, of course, except in the cathartic feeling of superiority that the lucid must experience when they realize the absence of patent answers.

It is precisely this painful phenomenon of growing up, of aging, that makes of Marguerite Duras' characters classic person-ages mirroring our own anxieties and dilemmas. Poirot-Delpech, noted critic of *Le Monde,* pointed out that the dramatist "possesses the art of letting us see what secret yearnings lie beneath these casual words"[7] of "La Musica." And the public's enthusiastic reception of the play bears the critic out. For the longings of Anne-Marie and Michel permeate and move readers and spectators alike. We feel compelled to share theirs and to allow our own to come forth from the placid storehouse we use to tuck conveniently away the frustration and privation of daily existence. The following lines at the end of the dramatic dia-logue summarize the uncertainty Anne-Marie and Michel, like most of us, must go on facing, permanently, even after the exhaustive effort of communicating with frankness and candor on problems others manage to take for granted and live with comfortably:

MICHEL: My wife. (*A long pause*) Will we see each other again?
ANNE-MARIE: I don't know.
MICHEL: But if this should ever come to be?
ANNE-MARIE: I don't know.
MICHEL: But if ever you and I, once more . . .
ANNE-MARIE: Then we shall die, undoubtedly, as lovers do.
MICHEL: What is going on?
ANNE-MARIE: When?
MICHEL: Now. Is it the beginning or the end?
ANNE-MARIE: Who knows?

Who knows whether or not the couple will reunite; whether or not a reunion is feasible or desirable; whether or not the same scenes and dramas they had spoken of earlier, would recur, with the same or a greater intensity and frequency? *La Musica* answers plainly: no one—which makes it all the more imperative to ask the questions.

While it is apparent that *Les Eaux et forêts* is a play of uneven quality, *Les Viaducs de la Seine-et-Oise* and "La Musica" especially, have been well received and have placed Margurite Duras, the novelist, in the enviable limelight of a playwright of repute. In fact, *Théâtre I* has established her ability to transfer successfully to the stage, in the tighter and more difficult format the theater requires, the same, basic, human and humane preoccupations so lucidly exposed in her novels. William H. Bowen's comment on *Théâtre I*—"none of her novels has been dramatized"[8]—is as erroneous in fact as is his earlier assertion: "Although one of the best-known French novelists of today, Marguerite Duras is seldom thought of as a writer for the theater";[9] and those who are more familiar with the author's plays and criticism thereof can accept neither.

The theater of Madame Duras actually occupies an increasingly major portion of the writer's output: besides the three original plays discussed above, the two adaptations of previously published works and two of works by American authors,[10] *Théâtre II* which appeared in 1968, contained four new plays and the dramatic version of *Des Journées entières dans les arbres*. In addition, *L'Amante anglaise*, the play version of the novel by the same title (itself a reworking of *Les Viaducs de la Seine-et-Oise*) was presented on the stage in 1969.

V   Suzanna Andler

The first of the plays in *Théâtre II, Suzanna Andler*, is another love story. Not unlike "La Musica," with which it shares a number of themes, this short, four-act drama has not yet been presented on the stage. The reviewer almost wishes it had been, for then he might have been spared the awkward, difficult reading it provides, mainly because of the numberless stage directions which the author considers necessary as a complement to the dialogue.

The heroine named in the title is a woman in her forties, wife of a rich man with periodic extramarital affairs. Having come to the conclusion that she is "one of the most deceived women of Saint-Tropez," she decides to take a lover, a younger man,

Michel, himself married and a friend of her husband. The other two characters in the play, a real estate man, Rivière, and Monique Combès, Suzanna's girl friend and former mistress of Monsieur Andler, are, like Michel and the heroine, members of the "jet set," egocentrics whose lack of financial worries provides them with a great deal of free time in which to travel, drink, and engage in loveless liaisons. But Suzanna and her husband, Jean, are also compassionate, sensitive persons, capable of understanding each other at times, even of loving one another, in spite of distance or of another's company, and in spite of the physical pleasure they find, apparently, in someone else's arms. This is particularly evident in the third act, which consists exclusively of a telephone conversation between husband and wife. There is, in the words and the tone used, a reciprocal desire not to hurt one another, and above all a tenderness that betrays fondness if not love. Jean and Suzanna are careful about remaining free from recrimination, about sparing each other's feelings but without engendering false illusions on what the future might still hold for their marriage.

While *Le Square* had dealt with the problems of acquaintanceship between Man and Woman, and "La Musica" with the relationship between a divorced couple, *Suzanna Andler* appears to tackle the difficulties of a husband and wife about to separate but still clinging, desperately, to the last bonds that remain between them. His mistress and her lover do not manage to effect the total atmosphere of indifference to the past and excitement about the possibility of a new life that would be required for an official divorce. The two seem, on the contrary, to seek one another in the very person to whom they have become extra-legally attached. Michel, clever and cunning, notices this and, cruel and bitter about the whole situation, he points to Suzanna that it is only through her husband that he can hurt her. "In this world," he concludes, "you only suffer for him." On the other hand, Jean's willingness to "accommodate" his wife (he even agrees to rent a very expensive villa for her, knowing that this is where she will spend her time with Michel), his solicitous attitude during the long telephone conversation of Act III, his offers to fly out to see her, his admonition to Michel not to hurt Suzanna, ever, indicate a position which is hardly compatible with the idea of definitive separation.

And so, it appears that, like Anne-Marie Roche and Michel Nollet of "La Musica," Jean and Suzanna have fallen into the *trap* of deceiving one another for the same reason: the necessity of breaking the routine by seeking the unknown. To Jean's question "What is going to become of us?" Suzanna's painful, reluctant answer (it comes only after a long pause) is: "I am going to rejoin him [her lover]." Perhaps, then, husband and wife will fall completely out of love; perhaps they will lose that feeling of tenderness and fondness which still unites them; perhaps divorce will follow. The last piece of dialogue in the play is not any more conclusive than the final scene of "La Musica." Trying to define their own relationship and to look into their own future, Suzanna and Michel close the drama as follows:

SUZANNA: A love . . . unlivable? An agony?
MICHEL: Yes. (*Pause.*) No matter what kind . . . another love is more attractive than this one [the one between a husband and wife].
SUZANNA, *opaque*: Perhaps we love each other . . .
MICHEL: Perhaps we do love each other.
SUZANNA: Yes? Perhaps? (*Pause.*) Perhaps I do love you.

Just as in "La Musica," the future of the two main characters remains an open question, so too in *Suzanna Andler*, it is impossible to anticipate the outcome of the search, of the probing, of the groping of heroes and heroines for solutions to unexplained and unexplainable but very real problems. One cannot love permanently one's spouse, Marguerite Duras seems to reiterate, nor can one duplicate, in extramarital affairs, the earlier moments of passion one has known. Love, like life because it is life, can only touch human beings temporarily and ephemerally, disappearing all too soon but not before leaving an indelible, an incurable cicatrice which is both a blessing and a curse.

Like the previously discussed drama, *Suzanna Andler* has very few of the characteristics usually associated with an anti-play: there is a plot, the personages are immediately recognizable, and their lucidity makes the dialogue easily accessible. On the other hand, the characters' repeated use of the word "perhaps," Suzanna's inability to recall exactly for how long she has been more or less separated from her husband (at one point she seems to think that it is five years, at another seven, still at another nine) and her difficulty in knowing what she wants, point

still to a vague connection with the themes and preoccupations
of anti-dramatists. Be this as it may, *Suzanna Andler* impresses
less than the earlier and the more compact "La Musica." The
reworking of a somewhat similar plot under a second title is
not a wise choice for any playwright, not even for one with
as much dramatic flair as Marguerite Duras.

VI *"Yes, peut-être"*

The author's fifth original play was first presented on the
stage in January 1968 and subsequently positioned third in
Théâtre II, following the dramatic version of *Des Journées
entières dans les arbres.* The author herself staged the production of this curious little one-act piece.

The two main characters, A and B, female, talk cryptically
about an *object* A has dragged onto the stage, an exhausted
soldier, a survivor from another world, from a militaristic society
bent on destroying itself and dead now, subject to the derision of
the two women. Throughout the dialogue, B asks the questions
and A supplies the answers. The beginning directions specify
that their voice must be identical and that the two women must
appear "innocent, insolent, tender and gay, without sadness, with-
out malice, without amiability without intelligence without stu-
pidity, without references, without memory." The only recollection they still have is that of words; not in proper syntactic construction, to be sure, nor benefiting from regular punctuation.
Moreover, the absence of personal pronouns in their speech de-
humanizes the people they refer to and themselves also, and
renders history extremely blurred and obscure. Both women,
however, carry a Geiger counter, and they seem determined to
go on living in spite of the catastrophic events whose memory
they have lost, for the most part, but whose radioactive conse-
quence persists, painful and permanent.

The third character, nameless, dormant, periodically fainting
because of the fatigue, is a semi-living relic of "the *bad* old
days." In the year 3000 one no longer knows what to do with
soldiers, with slogans, with propaganda. A and B are, also, thoroughly puzzled by his appearance. His torn clothes, marked by
such inscriptions as "honor" "fatherland," "*God*" (the latter word
is in English and the italics are the author's), have sewn on

them a number of stars of the American flag, the emblem of the
Legion of Honor, and other signs or adages arranged so as to
paraphrase or relate to the well-known advertising catchwords
of Dubonnet wine, the Scandale brand of girdles, and so on.
From time to time, we are told, the man is supposed to hum a
military march or the national hymn of the country in which
the play is presented. Yet, some of the stage directions, as well
as several English words used by A and B, suggest perhaps that
Marguerite Duras did not simply want to deride war in general,
as in "Yes, peut-être," but that she may have had in mind America's involvement in South Vietnam, a topic of considerable
interest to many French intellectuals around the time of the play's
production: "Used to go," A tells B. "To return, To get settled
[in a given country]. To burn. To kill, To escalate. Used to
go to the Asiaticos where never seen before, used to say they
were defending the motherland." The following bit of dialogue
also seems, further, to mock our dependence on often useless
gadgets and our concern with our lack of history:

A: . . . Some stones with inscriptions on them were found around
here.
B: Oh?
A: Call them *non historical silex* [the writer underlines these words
since she uses English].
This is an allusion to American gadgets [the italics are the author's].
B: But what does that mean?
A: That nothing happened.
B: Inscriptions whose purpose is to say that nothing happened?
A: Yes. From this year to that year: *nothing.*
B, *repeats: Nothing.*

But other materialistic societies are mocked as well, that of
Germany for example, in A's recollection: "Used to say: Uber
Alles Enfants d'Patrie," followed by the stage indication "*Said
as enfant d'putain.*" And religious societies too, are derided,
for A appears to think that all evil stems from God since it is He
who inspired Man with an uncontrollable need for masters,
divine and human; and the situation got to the point where
people could not do without:

A: All: used to seek masters. Saw them everywhere, wanted
masters, masters, wanted them, wanted them.

B: O lala, why masters, masters?

A: So that could get kicked in the ass by them. (*Pause. Suave.*) Used to adore that.

And the masters' appetite for war resulted in their present loneliness (there are only three survivors) and in the desert mentioned in the following comico-pathetic dialogue:

A: Used to say: "Our *God* who are in Heaven give us our daily ration."

B: And le *God* what did use to say?

A: Used to say: "Wait wait."

B, *laughs*: And did send it?

A: Nails, it seems. (*In the literal sense, gesture pointing to her behind.*) It's funny.

B: O lala, something like that is funny.

A: Funny, *yes!* (*Mysterious and grave all of a sudden.*) Waited for thousands and thousands of years.

B: What?

A, *pointing to the desert*: That.

B, *suddenly frightened*: It's funny, *yes.*

A: Funny, *yes.*

B, *pause, lively tone*: Were stupid or what, the people before us?

A: Neither more nor less stupid than are, say. The more stupid were on top.

B: On top of what?

A: Of the less stupid, say.

Marguerite Duras' irreverence is here stronger than in "Madame Dodin," than in any previous work. Yet, this need not have a shocking effect, especially since the words and gestures are those of personages a thousand years into the future. In addition, the comicality of this and other similar passages draws the spectator's attention away from the more serious and more controversial ideas of the author. Marguerite Duras' humor is especially original in "Yes peut-être," for here she appears to have been able to depart radically from the expected use of language and to introdnce the innovation of omitting personal pronouns as well as a rather Rabelaisian-type of verve in strange, puzzling, often antithetical vocabulary combinations ("B: Good morning, good evening," for example) and in the introduction of nonexistent words: "A: 'Were thinkers before. All: great thinkers." B, *flat*: Oh. *Pause.*) '*Pensivaient* what?'"

Jacques Lemarchand, noted critic of *Le Figaro Littéraire,* did not like, however, Marguerite Duras' attempt "to ridicule war."[11] While admitting that the idea of the discovery of a soldier, still partly functioning, by people of the year 3000 who no longer know what war is, could have been interesting, he deplores the fact that the dialogue goes on and on, that the characters engage in a number of depressing naïvetés, and that the diction imposed on the actors by the writer (who, it will be remembered, staged the play) was difficult to listen to because of the repeated hiccups of A and B and the hard, noisy breathing of the soldier. Although Madame Duras' debut as directress may leave something to be desired, it is difficult nevertheless to accept the other two criticisms of Jacques Lemarchand: the dialogue does not drag since the play is very short; and the naïvetés of the heroines are largely explained by their loss of memory of the events to which they refer. Actually, "Yes, peut-être" is, for the reader at least, a most enjoyable play. The originality of the situation and the singularity of the language would perhaps be sufficient for a good dramatic composition. But there is, also, the mixture of humor and tragedy in the efforts of A and B to recall, to reconstruct, to understand. And there is, as in so many previous works of Marguerite Duras, a reiteration of the necessity to try to go on living: for neither loneliness, nor the desert, nor the inconvenience of walking around with Geiger counters can deter the two women from believing in the importance of life. Their low intelligence notwithstanding, and in spite of the paucity of means at their disposal, the incarnation of A and B through steadfast doggedness makes survival passable and palatable. *Je* and *vous* have disappeared, of course, but there remains a sisterhood of fear and defeat even after the catastropic events which have almost ended the world.

VII *"Le Shaga"*

Presented on a double bill with "Yes, peut-être," and also benefiting from the stage direction of the author, "Le Shaga" tells the story of two women, A and B again, and of a man, called simply H. The public is informed at the outset that, perhaps, the meeting place of the three characters is the courtyard of a mental hospital. When the curtain rises, A discovers that B has forgotten how to speak French and has adopted as means of communication another language, the Shaga. B's first remarks are translated by the author in parenthesis, her later speeches being then understood by A who translates them for the benefit of H; as the play progresses, however, and whenever he wishes to, H is quite capable of understanding the new-old language without anyone's help. On the stage, the gestures, the context and, at times, the curious similarities between Shaga and French, make comprehension possible, if not altogether easy.

The brief description of the play on the jacket of *Théâtre II* informs us that, in spite of the unknown language, the three personages manage, nevertheless, to converse with one another. This is an acceptable interpretation, perhaps, but even then conversation must be defined very loosely. What do A, B, and H talk about? The weather, at first; themselves, but without clear knowldege of the past and often in contradictory terms; a gas can with holes in it (H explains that he is here because he has run out of gas—it happened two years ago); a trip H took once to Monte Carlo; and a mysterious bird whose story H narrates or attempts to narrate, the starting point of the story being sometime in the middle, sometime at the end, but never at the beginning. The dialogue is often interrupted by laughter, hearty, noisy, unconvincing laughter, and by comic interludes akin to farce: itching, which contaminates all characters; scratching in unison; the uttering and repeating of strange, theatrially effective sounds in Shaga, sounds which are close to many in French and in Latin; and, finally, the alternation of short and longer speeches at speeds varying from very slow to very fast. These devices give the play a certain movement, and the amateurs of farce can perhaps find a certain amount of satisfaction in the comings and goings of lunatics or semidemented personages who mimic life.

Jacques Lemarchand, however, already ill-disposed toward the dramatist after viewing "Yes, peut-être," the first of the plays on the double bill, accuses the writer of a return, in "Le Shaga," to a familiar language, that already used by Molière in *Le Bourgeois gentilhomme* (1670) and in *Le Malade imaginaire* (1673); and he implies that there is, then, little originality in her comedy, and not much else to speak of.[12] But all French comedy-writers are related to Molière, and his influence, when found, is perhaps more to the credit than to the debit of the author who did not shake it. Significant to a greater extent is the rather obvious recollection of Ionesco in many of the speeches in the play: for the words of Shaga are not unlike the curious utterances in such comedies as *Jacques ou la soumission* (1955) or *L'Avenir est dans les oeufs* (1955) of the *Roi des absurdes*. Marguerite Duras' reminisces of Ionesco can also be seen in the unwillingness of A to accept the principle of contradiction and in her reception of like statements which she interprets as opposing. The following passage is an example: "This doesn't mean that it arrives on its left foot from historical depths. It means something else. That it arrives on its left foot from historical depths, it means only one thing, that it arrives on its left foot from historical depths, nothing else." The very comico-tragic scene in which A questions B on her past, with the latter's repetition of the one-word reply: *"Terminé"* (finished), the only French word she still remembers, is likewise an Ionesco-type of *trouvaille* and deserves quotation here in spite of its length:

A: And your husband? Is he there to look at you, your husband?

B: Finished my husband. Finished my husband.

H: My, my . . .

A: . . . And the children, come now, the children, after all?

B, *Shaga accent*: Finished, finished.

A: But after all . . . your apartment? (*Faster and faster.*) Your organization? Your receptions? Your relations?

B: Finished, finished.

A: And your country? Your country? Europe, after all? Europe?

B: Finished, Finished.

A: And values? Your patrimony? The Parthenon? The Pataguas? The popes, the papas, the steps [the word in French is *pas*], the popes?

B: Finished, finished.

A: Alsatia? (*Pause.*) And Lorraine, what about them? (*Pause.*) Say, what about Lorraine?

B: Finished, finished.

A: Saint-Peter and Miquelon? The castles, the castles? Brest, Brest?

B: Finished, finished.

A. Venice, Notre-Dame of Venice, what about them? And the gas and the electricity?

B: Finished.

Sudden stop. Moment of immobility. Then they burst out in laughter and begin to dance a sort of Charleston on a Cambodian tune.

A decade or so before the date of Marguerite Duras' play, in his heyday, Ionesco had managed to get an international reputation with dramatic dialogues of this genre. But often what is a reaction becomes all too soon an *école,* and "Le Shaga" did not receive any of the public adulation bestowed upon the writer's predecessor. Spectators and readers have grown weary perhaps; and the many comico-sad commentaries in the passage quoted notwithstanding, "Le Shaga" failed, and Marguerite Duras was obliged to acquiesce: "If the play is going to have the significance that I expect it to have, perhaps it will not be immediately.[13] There is a bit of optimism on the part of the dramatist, but it is difficult to see how the future might hold the key to "Le Shaga's" success. Its themes and preoccupations are not new and are not going to rejuvenate. Others had explored them better in previous works of a higher degree of inventiveness.

That is not to say that "Le Shaga" is altogether a bad composition. When she relies on her own originality, the playwright's pen becomes painlessly effective. For example, recalling one of the more notable scenes in "Les Eaux et forêts" when Man boasts about his real or imaginary possessions, Marguerite Duras also has A enumerate past, true or false assets:

I had already many advantages . . . A house, a husband, children, a personality, an automobile, a situation, a certain maturity, a name, two automobiles, a reputation, a dog, an education, a country, a homeland . . . a life . . . a furcoat, a religion, thirty-years-old, thirty-one a furcoat, thirty-two, thirty-three, thirty-four two furcoats thirty-five four lovers . . . thirty-six, thirty-seven, I told myself: a lion. That's what I need . . . I had it. He'd say nothing. He roared. 547 kilograms. Six kilograms of meat a day. One has to have the means, alright, I had them. . . . He became a weakling. We were separated.

Like Man of the previous play, A boasts of things she had or would have liked to have; and the demise of the lion (standing perhaps for her husband) points, as Man's final confession in "Les Eaux et forêts," to the disappearance of all the assets of the character. In the case of A, however, there is the additional pathos of the loss of reason following that of things and beings.

But this very fact, that she and the others have become demented, places "Le Shaga" among those generally successful plays about lunatics.[14] Such plays, whatever their other faults or qualities, deal with characters who, because they are irresponsible, can allow themselves to express thoughts and desires that the sane can only dream of in the utmost secrecy. When the personages of "Le Shaga" do this, small bits of dialogue can very well entice and seize the audience. The following is one example of many which could be offered: "H: What would you like to know? A, *in one breath*: All-how-and-why. And because." The point is that, in her state of lunacy, A is further from her goal than persons who are still in full or partial possession of their reason. Yet, her all-or-nothing type of spiritual hunger casts upon her an aura of purity reminiscent of Jean Anouilh's Joan of Arc or Antigone. That is not to say that A, B and H remain tragic characters at odds with the world and ultimately crushed by it; because of their insanity they are in a peculiarly advantageous position; they are at the same time deeply involved and totally detached, which makes it possible for them to forget their predicaments and to begin to laugh or dance. This the reasonable cannot do, that is, he can neither go after the impossible, nor take failure in his stride. And so, through gestures and words, the characters on stage impart their *strength* and their *freedom* to the less audacious and more entrapped spectator. Viewed in this fashion, "Le Shaga" could make for satisfactory viewing.

VIII   Un Homme est venu me voir

Marguerite Duras' last published play is a disappointment. The plot, built around two survivors of a squabble between members of a Communist party, is meager and, in general, does not possess the gripping qualities of previous Durasian dramatic compositions. Steiner, a man in his late forties, married, middle class, and modestly satisfied with his middle-of-the-road bourgeois status, receives the unexpected visit of a former comrade named, appropriately enough, Visitor. Eighteen years ago the two men had held opposing political views. Steiner had lost, was imprisoned, escaped, and subsequently had managed to make a new life for himself. He is now free from political entanglements and can afford a quiet existence which incorporates

money, two cars, children, trips. Visitor, whose party faction
was in power for a while, saw his fortunes diminish and ultimately disappear: new men and new ideas insinuated themselves among the leaders, and he was reduced to the lowest of
the fallen states. "My disgrace was total," he confesses. "I cleaned
the offices of the others, the new ones, I became their *femme de
chambre* . . . I became their errand boy. From morning till
night on my bike, I carried confidential letters. . . . I have no
ideas except those parallel to the ones I am supposed to have.
I live with my eyes half shut. I submit. I keep quiet. I am never
for, nor against. I listen to everything. I must listen, otherwise
I would be charged with lack of interest." Visitor's lucid examination of his *fall* is, however, just stoic enough to preclude the
spectator's sympathy. He accepts the degeneration of his position, as Steiner approves of the *rise* of his. Unlike previous Durasian characters who engaged in real fights and obtained at least
a utopian reincarnation, the two personages of "Un Homme est
venu me voir" are content with making a cold review of the facts
which have led to the situation in which they find themselves
at present.

Their dialogue is perhaps too intelligent: it is philosophical in
tone, penetrating in analysis. Yet, it often seizes and summar-
izes in catchy, little sentences the many unsolvable problems of
human existence. "At first it was too soon," notes Visitor, pointing to the difficulty of timing. "And then too late." And Steiner
also, Steiner the more passive of the two, the more satisfied,
the more bourgeois, states, with momentary spite but also with
cold-bloodedness, that "what is needed, what is needed, you see,
is a return to the beginning, throw all men to the dogs, all of
them, and let humanity be born all over again." But these and
similar remarks appear to impress without touching. Steiner
and his guest do not have the sensitivity of other Durasian characters. Their cerebral qualities prevent them from suffering.
Spectators and readers can at best take a mild interest in their
general comments, but there is little participation in their
specific problems, little identification with the heroes on the
stage. For the two former friends seem to be consoled by the
fact that what has happened to them has happened to others
and will happen to others, in fact to everyone, always:

VISITOR, *turning away from Steiner, facing the public*: For ten years, body and soul we devoted ourselves to the same cause. Fraternally.

STEINER: Yes.

VISITOR: And then, one day, two different currents emerged.

STEINER, *like a somnambulist*: That's it, yes . . .

VISITOR, *goes on, in clear, oratory fashion*: We were separated. (*Pause.*) You were on one side, I on the other. (*Pause.*) You on the side of the guilty. I on the side of the powerful: this is the way it has been throughout history.

And the idea that in the universal melting pot all persons and things are of equal, unimportant value, is added at the end of the play when Visitor ceases perhaps completely to care: "History will cover us with the same evil, we shall be the contemporaries of one and the same error, and the respective parts that we have played, in their eyes will be no different at all: all our sins will equal each other . . . you that of having allowed yourself to be beaten, we that of having conquered."

It appears, then, that the personages of "Un Homme est venu me voir" start and end their encounter at a point where most previous characters of Marguerite Duras, fatigued and partly or totally defeated, decide to abandon the struggle and accept the mediocrity of existence. But the latter had fought in the interim, had made certain gestures, had even caught a glimpse, from time to time, of modest, modified happiness; and spectators and readers were made witness to the struggles, to the partial or utopian successes. Steiner's and Visitor's struggles, on the other hand, occurred only in the past. The characters on the stage do not evolve, their present and their future is one and the same. And their carefully reasoned outlook on life spares them the constrictions of the usually fragile human sensitivity. But it is one thing not to witness any real change, any real experience; it is another not to witness any pain.

IX *Summary*

Théâtre II is, then, an undertaking of uneven results. With the exception of the much-acclaimed *Des Journées entières dans les arbres,* the plays have met with modest success only, at times, as in the case of "Yes, peut-être" and "Le Shaga," with a certain amount of critical admonition. *Théâtre II* contains little that compares with the forceful *Viaducs de la Seine-et-Oise* or with the intriguing "La Musica." In general, however, Marguerite Duras' dramas retain the novelist's ability to weave hauntingly pathetic situations under the guise of incoherent plots, unimportant details and banal conversations. But her pessimism with regard to the human condition borders on without matching the despair to be found in other contemporary playwrights. And we can detect in her plays "the immense attention [she pays] to her personages and even a secret tenderness."[15] For, as the critic concludes, "Marguerite Duras feels for her characters, somewhat as God does for his sinners."[16]

CHAPTER 6

The Films

I Hiroshima, mon amour

IT is no exaggeration to say that, more than any other work, *Hiroshima, mon amour* has established the international reputation of Madame Duras. It is not merely the fact that the movie has received the International Critics Prize at the Cannes Film Festival in 1959 and the New York Film Critics Award in 1960; it is more the popularity of this work of art in countless countries throughout the world, popularity with the elite and with the average moviegoer, which has made of it an unqualified success. The usually unsafe barometer of box-office receipts, added to the official acclaim, is proof, in this case, that a finely nuanced and authentically wrought screen portrait can be pleasing to both the intelligentsia and the mass audiences of many a nation.

The story of a nameless French actress who meets and falls in love with a nameless Japanese architect the day before she is supposed to return to France is a banal story, perhaps better known in this country than any other Durasian narration. The chance encounter between a married woman and a married man, and the resulting brief but passionate love affair, are supplemented artfully by the engaging dialogue between the two, by the woman's interior monologues and the skillful alternation of views of contemporary Hiroshima with flashbacks of the town of Nevers during World War II. The initial scene, with the two protagonists' naked bodies filling the cinema screen, is particularly effective. She tells him that she has familiarized herself with everything in Hiroshima. And he contradicts her, maintaining that she saw nothing. We see what she has seen; the mutilated bodies, the dead fish on the beaches, the pictures in the museum depicting the aftermath of the atomic attack. And then we see the beautifully intact shape of the two lovers, the smoothness of their flesh, the deliberate slowness of their volup-

tuous embraces. "You saw nothing in Hiroshima," he persists,
and we get the point, that it is impossible to talk about what
happened, that it is impossible to imagine what happened, that it
is impossible to identify with the pain or the feelings of the
survivors. All one can do is to talk about these impossibilities.
And the pounding repetitions in her speech underline the un-
shakable impotence of those who were not there, and their
guilt for not having been there: "Four times at the museum of
Hiroshima. . . . Among the photographs, the photographs, the
reconstructions, for want of something else, the explanations,
for want of something else . . . the burned iron. The broken iron,
the iron made vulnerable as flesh. . . . Human skin floating. . . .
Burned stones. Shattered stones. Anonymous heads of hair
that the women of Hiroshima, when they awoke in the morning,
discovered had fallen out. . . . Ten thousand degrees at Peace
Square. . . . The temperature of the sun at Peace Square. . . ."

There is something incantatory about the words spoken, not
only when they describe the horrors of Hiroshima but throughout the scenario, especially those uttered during the lovemaking
scenes. Her exhortations to him are poetry: in tone, in content,
in the way they appear in print in the book version:

Who are you?
You destroy me.
You're so good for me.
How could I have known that this city was made to the size of love?
How could I have known that you were made to the size of my body?
You're great. How wonderful. You're great.
How slow all of a sudden.
And how sweet.
More than you can know.
You destroy me.
You're so good for me.
You destroy me.
You're so good for me.
Plenty of time.
Please.
Take me.
Deform me, make me ugly. . . .

What is noteworthy in the passage quoted is not only the
hauntingly bewitching quality of hero and heroine reaching

out for love, but a theme often encountered in the works of
Marguerite Duras: the possibility, in spite of insuperable odds,
of making contact, for a brief moment, of striving toward a
measure of understanding, no matter how fragile, of enjoying,
even of taking delight, in fleeting fashion, of certain flashes of
real existence. For although they are a world apart, geographic-
ally, racially, and philosophically, and although they are drawn
even further apart by the fact that they are both married, and
by the fact that they both have children, and by the fact that
she must, unavoidably, return to France next day, there is still
her power to make him listen, and his to change her, to make
believe that he can reincarnate this woman (as the Man in
Le Square was unable to do, at least during the course of the
novel) whom he had chosen and who implores him at one
time: "Deform me to your likeness." Of course, there is only a
temporary change (that effected during the time of actual
intercourse), and a utopian one at that; and there is no reincarnation. For their complete love is also a hopeless love, killed
even before the initial contact, because of the previously legal-
ized obligations, because of the prior commitments. That is not
to say, however, that their meeting is useless. Like the citizens
of Hiroshima who refuse to lie down and die in spite of the
catastrophe, like the "women who risk giving birth to malformed
children, to monsters, but it goes on," like the "men who risk
becoming sterile, but it goes on," the French actress and the
Japanese architect can have a go at the impossible, can look
at each other and talk to each other and establish a doomed but
very real and very rupturous rapport. Marguerite Duras points
out in her own synopsis of the film that it is true that in the
end the two characters "are reduced to a terrifying, mutual
impotence";[1] yet, as she had commented just before in the same
synopsis, because their love is killed and "therefore already relegated to oblivion, [it is] therefore eternal."[2]

But *Hiroshima, mon amour* is not just a love story, nor simply
an antiwar movie; it is also, as the back cover of the Grove
edition of the scenario reminds us, "a Proustian creation of re-
membrance." The narration of what had happened at Nevers
fifteen years earlier,—the story of a young girl falling in love
with a German soldier of the forces of occupation, of their brief
and guilt-ridden liaison, of his assassination at the hands of the

guerillas just before the liberation, of the shaving of her head as punishment for having loved an enemy, of her subsequent hiding in the cellar of her home,—provides for pathetic scenes which she depicts for the Japanese, horrifying in their own way, even though they refer only to a banal wartime drama. The clever shifting of the cameras from Hiroshima to Nevers and back to Hiroshima adds to the poignancy of the narration. The heroine points out that only when the bomb was dropped on Hiroshima was she presentable enough to come out of the hiding place and to resume life. Her return to a seminormal existence coincided, then, with the unerasable marring of the human conscience which the attack implanted on mankind for all eternity. And the fact that one does not die of love, the fact that one survives, goes on, works, grows, laughs, and loves all over again and in spite of whatever else happens in the world, are realities which determine one's life and explain one's future actions and reactions. Marguerite Duras elucidates:

It's not the fact of having been shaved and disgraced that marks her life, it's the already mentioned defeat: the fact that she didn't die of love on August 2, 1944, on the banks of the Loire.

This is not in contradiction with her attitude at Hiroshima with the Japanese. On the contrary, this has a direct bearing on her attitude with the Japanese. . . . What she tells the Japanese is this lost opportunity which has made her what she is.

The story she tells of this lost opportunity literally transports her outside herself and carries her toward this new man.[3]

The above provides the answer to questions raised by the author in the film's synopsis: "What happened in Nevers? . . . What happened to make her the way she is, so free and yet so haunted, so honest and yet so dishonest, so equivocal and so clear? So predisposed to chance love affairs?"[4] What happened was, of course, her survival: survival after the death of the German soldier, survival after Hiroshima. And the guilt that goes with it, and the need to expose oneself, over and over again, even in the course of chance meetings, even at the expense of moral or civil laws, in order to reassert that vulnerability which was spared on previous occasions. Masochism, of course, is in all this, but perhaps there is a certain liberating feeling which compensates for it and gives the illusion of reincarnation. Anonymous pawns in an unexplainable and inimical universe, She and He acquire indeed, at the end of the story, an identity, a name, an essence:

SHE: Hi-ro-shi-ma.
Hi-ro-shi-ma. That's your name.
(*They look at each other without seeing each other. Forever.*)
HE: That's my name. Yes. Your name is Nevers. Ne-vers—in France.

Their respective essence is, then, that of their native town and, by extension, that of their country and of the different world they represent. For in them and through them there was a meeting, an understanding, a fusion of two societies with nothing in common, with everything in common. And their love, devoid of promises, of hope, of vows, appears pure because it is freely undertaken, with full consciousness of the risks and of the inevitability of separation; and it is eternal because it transcends the lovers, just as it is eternal because it is doomed.[5]

The critical adulations brought upon *Hiroshima, mon amour* have been numerous and almost always stated in superlative terms. On the occasion of Gallimard's publication of the scenario in book form, Maryvonne Butcher wrote: "To be able to read the actual words of Hiroshima, to savour the reiteration of the phrases, to study the cadences in their relation to the unforgettable images, to see how precisely the Proustian flow of time has been indicated by the utmost economy of word and camera-movement is to understand the subtlety of the film as never before."[6] This criticism should be consoling to those who have not been fortunate enough to see what may very well be the most remarkable motion picture landmark of the century.

II Une Aussi longue absence

Marguerite Duras' second scenario was written in collaboration with Gérard Jarlot, friend and novelist[7] whom she confessed having consulted also for the text of *Hiroshima, mon amour*.[8] It is difficult to determine to what extent each of the two authors has contributed to the dialogue of *Une Aussi longue absence*: Jarlot's other publications reveal a kinship with most of Madame Duras' themes, and there is, also, much that is similar in the style and format of their stories. The professional connection between the two has been close, and on several occasions

Marguerite Duras has acknowledged her debt to the lucid and sensitive suggestions of her colleague.

Une Aussi longue absence has been crowned with the 1961 Palme d'Or prize at the Cannes Film Festival. The work, however, did not attain the international reputation of *Hiroshima, mon amour,* nor was it, in France itself, so popular as its predecessor. It is not a "thousand films in one," as *Hiroshima* was often called. It has a limited plot which deals with the banal, frequently encountered situation of a man suffering from amnesia. Albert Langlois had fallen into the hands of the Gestapo in 1944, was tortured, deported, later released and turned loose into the world. But his memory became lost somewhere along the way, during one of the beatings in France, or in the cencentration camp in Germany. Sixteen years later, Thérèse, his wife, occupies a modestly successful position in society: she is the owner of a thriving restaurant; she is a stable businesswoman; she has a steady lover. But one day she recognizes her husband in the person of a bum.[9] And from that point on the story follows a familiar course: there is her attempt to restore his memory, his inability to respond, her perseverance, his refusal to understand or to recognize his wife and, finally, his disappearance.

Unlike the previous film in which both the dialogue and the author's notations and directions were of considerable importance, *Une Aussi longue absence* betrays the preoccupations of the writers more through their interventions in the text than through the shorter, less revealing conversations of the protagonists. These interventions describe the outer and inner makeup of the characters. We learn, for example, that the beautiful and charming thirty-eight-year-old Thérèse, who has forgotten her husband and has made a new life for herself, like so many previous Durasian females, has only accepted a compromise, an existence *on the rebound,* as it were. Her busy routine as restaurant owner, her lack of financial worries, her sexually satisfying liaison with Pierre, are so many pills and palliatives affording a passably pleasing sense of living. But the chance encounter with Albert dispels the illusion of satisfaction. The long-standing affair with Pierre is over, the restaurant itself begins to be neglected, and she spends all her time trying, ultimately in vain, to achieve some sort of reincarnation through a return to her first love and her first commitment. This is obvious in the description of her reaction to Albert's admission of his loss of memory: *"Thérèse is stretched out on the bench. She has lost conscious-ness. Hearing the last sentence of the hobo, she has fainted. . . . Her fainting, so long so simple . . . was an immense fainting. A 'living death' out of which a love story will be born. She comes out of it 'disfigured,' transformed for all eternity. She is resusci-tated in the certitude and the youthfulness of love."*

But this is how things appear only. For as the title of the scenario suggests, the absence has been too long, and it is much too late. Somewhat like the heroine of *Le Marin de Gibraltar*, she pursues Albert Langolis through the streets, in the alley-ways, in all the hangouts he frequents or she thinks he frequents. Yet, these pursuits, cinematographic as they may be (the authors indicate that they must be "animated like a Western"), remain futile even when she manages to catch up with him; for there is practically no communication between the two. The long scene in which she watches her husband trying to untie, patiently, methodically, and with the greatest care, the twenty-five knots of the string around a bundle of old magazines (which he prob-ably intends to sell), is one of the most effective of the entire motion picture and one of the most revealing of this lack of com-munication. The writers' comments on this sequence inform us that here they *"have caught the hobo at the only thing which interests him truly and totally. Thus, it is quite natural that he pays no attention to Thérèse."* Actually, a little later on when she draws him into the restaurant and gives him what is the best present she could offer, a package of old magazines, Albert has to go once more through the process of untying knots and, once more, he fails to pay attention to his wife. Only this time there are as many as forty of them, and once he has untied them all he proceeds to tie them back, with the utmost care, so that the package is returned to the exact condition in which it was handed to him. And in a footnote to the description of all this the authors explain: "What we have wanted to show here is the absolutely invented, gratuitous but absorbing, passionate and methodic activity of this man. He exercises this activity like a professional; the only difference is that we do not perceive the aim of this activity." But of course, there are no aims in an absurd and inimical world, as those familiar with the works of anti-novelists already know. Marguerite Duras and Gérard Jarlot simply restate here the void of life and the mechanical routines with which we attempt to fill this void: themes already encountered in the former's and the latter's other works.

While presented much more often in the writers' interventions in the text, these themes appear also, on occasion, in the short dialogues betwen hero and heroine, in the difficult, almost impossible utterances which they manage, with the greatest effort, to address each other:

> THERESE: You could come, just like that . . . from time to time . . . (*Pause.*) We could see each other. (*Pause.*) Eat together once in a while . . . (*Pause.*) If you like to . . . We could talk . . . like this. (*Pause.*) Listen to some music. (*Pause.*) You . . . (*She stops abruptly.*)
> THE HOBO: It's just that I am very busy.

His wife, astonished at the fact that he is so busy doing nothing, asks, later on, what specifically his existence is like. And Albert, who wonders, inquires, searches, finds only very little to say: "I get up, I start to walk . . . and there. I get up, I walk, that's it . . . yes . . .I get up. I walk. Sometimes I get a headache. (*Gesture.*) There." Life is chaotic, the writers indicate, and cruel as well, for not only there is nothing worth doing, but one must do this *nothing* with patience and conviction; and always at the expense of something else, possible or impossible, at the expense of another way of living, of new ties or the renewal of old ones, to the point of physical and spiritual deterioration as suggested by the headache in Albert's reply. Actually, for him the absence has been so long that, when Thérèse attempts to show that it is possible to recover his memory, that one day doctors might find something, that it would be worth while, after all, he rejects even the idea of thinking about it. "Perhaps," she insists, "you used to have, before, homes, princely properties . . . the very best of friends . . . a wife . . . and perhaps adventures . . . who knows? Maybe you used to travel. To the end of the world . . . so, why refuse all that? A whole life might open up behind you . . . why turn it down?" But Albert does not understand; he remains quiet and finally walks away. In her last speech Thérèse still clings on to hope, however, and she tells Pierre: "Remember that in the winter, perhaps, when he is cold, perhaps he will re-

turn. . . . Summer is a bad season . . . (*Pause.*) While in winter
. . . not knowing where to go . . . I've got to wait for winter . . .
I've got to wait for winter . . ."

Waiting is the only solution, then, the only rampart against
the avalanche of total despair. It kept the Maid of *Le Square*
going, and so many other Durasian heroines, as it does readers
and spectators for whom the pathos of the characters' predicaments provides a cathartic feeling of security and temporary
safety.

III *Summary*

Marguerite Duras' original scenario, *Hiroshima mon amour*, as
well as the one she wrote in collaboration with Gérard Jarlot,
Une Aussi Longue absence, constitute, then, transpositions on
the cinema screen of topics close to the novelist's and the playwright's heart. While her first excursion in movie-writing has
been viewed by many as one of the finest examples of the
author's work, the second, more limited in scope, less ambitious
and certainly less poetic in tone, did not enjoy great popularity.
For Madame Duras, who had already used motion-picture techniques effectively in a number of novels,[10] the cinema was no
strange territory. Her flair for movement, for the clever shifting
of cameras, for the interplay of shadows and lights, and for the
construction of haunting dialogues, lent itself splendidly to
Hiroshima, mon amour, if somewhat less admirably to *Une Aussi
longue absence.* But it is not easy to duplicate a work of art
that comes very close to perfection; and Marguerite Duras did
well, perhaps, to entrust the film version of her own novels (*Le
Marin de Gibraltar, Moderato cantabile* and *Dix heures et demie
du soir en été*) to others, who did not have to live up to so
glorious a past as scenario writers.

CHAPTER 7

Conclusion

NOVELS, plays, and movie scenarios, these are the media through which Marguerite Duras has managed to obtain a considerable domestic and international fame. Having begun her writing career with two inconspicuous novels, she rose quickly on the French literary scene. Her initial flirt with the American-type fiction had betrayed an acute flair for anticipating the more difficult and the more serious preoccupations of her colleagues of later years, playwrights and novelists whose domain is aliterature or anti-literature. Yet, as the foregoing pages have shown (with the possible exception of *Les Chantiers* and *L'Après-midi de Monsieur Andesmas*), she has never given in entirely to all contemporary notions on the absurdity of life and the complete absence of the possibility of happiness. Remote, hidden, hardly traceable but invigorating and restating the dignity of the human condition, hope emerges, at times, from even the most despairing situations in which she places heroes and heroines.

Seekers of palliatives of debatable real or permanent value, her female characters especially, succumbing to liquor, to lust, to lovers, offer a vivid and touching example of the need to go on, to persist, to face the most insuperable odds with the most obstinate, if futile, stamina: Ma and her barriers against the Pacific, Anna and her quixotic search for the sailor from Gibraltar, Madame Dodin and her visions of the automation of garbage disposal systems, the Maid and her weekly attendance at a dance, and Maria's daring involvement in the life and death of Rodrigo Paestra are some of the more notable of the fictional personages and their efforts that fill the author's pages. These characters and their exertions remain alive in the memory of the reading public in spite of and because of their vulnerability. Likewise, in her plays and movie scenarios most females exhibit

154

an equal determination to resist the onslaught of permanent despair by means of attempts at activity and of endeavors to hold on to their minimal existence: the crime of Claire and the consolation she finds in Verdi's overture, the survival of A and B in spite of the impossible aftermath of the atomic war, the visions of A and B in "Le Shaga," the French actress' liaison with the Japanese in *Hiroshima, mon amour,* and Thérèse's vain hope in a future reunion with her hobo husband provide for cases in point.

Marguerite Duras' male characters, not always so clearly delineated, and possessing less vigor than their female counterparts, show nevertheless, on occasion, an ability for eluding, temporarily, the vicissitudes of their condition. This they do through a number of efforts: Nicolas' murder of his uncle in *La Vie tranquille,* for example, Gaston's naïve dreams and derisory liaison with Madame Dodin, Chauvin's emulation of the gestures of a murderer in *Moderato cantabile,* the French Vice-Consul's shooting of the dogs and lepers in the Shalimar Gardens, the phony enumeration of material and spiritual riches Man makes in "Les Eaux et forêts."

In her style, too, the author occupies a position which is only marginal with respect to that of the majority of writers of the New School. For example, she does not engage in the technical jargon of Robbe-Grillet; her phraseology is not nearly so cryptic as that of Nathalie Sarraute; and plots or fragments of plots are discernible in all her works. These middle-of-the-road stylistic procedures have been helpful in securing for her the sympathy of both the traditionally minded public and the attention of the more avant-garde reader. But there is more. If Marguerite Duras has been able to capture and to hold on to an international limelight it is mainly through the genuinely human sensitivity with which she endows heroes and heroines that she has done so. This sensitivity, no doubt, stems from her own very deep and very sedulous susceptibility to human bonds, to human needs, to human frailty, and to the devastating force of the myriad contradictory emotions that well within Man. But the ability of her characters to uncover minute and temporary joy remains cathartic for the reader, in spite of the limitations, the curbs, and the checks that bind and squeeze true existence out of personages that are ultimately acquiescing, ultimately resigned.

All this is not to say, however, that Marguerite Duras is a truly great author, one of unquestionable impact on the actions and reactions of contemporary *aficionados* of literature. She is no Sartre or Camus, no Simone de Beauvoir. As we have seen, she has had her detractors, and she is not free from a number of shortcomings: some manipulation of characters and events in the early novels, a return to an outmoded investigation of the phenomena of consciousness in *Le Ravissement de Lol V. Stein*, and, of late, a couple of rather mediocre plays. At age fifty-six Marguerite Duras remains a tireless writer, however, and it is doubtful that her period of greatest inspiration is over. But no matter what the future still holds for her career, now almost three decades long, it may be concluded that her contributions are such that her place in contemporary French letters is assured and her prominence is likely to survive. The unforgettable *Le Square*, *Moderato cantabile*, *Hiroshima, mon amour*, and "La Musica," among others, take the foregoing supposition out of the realm of prophecy and into that of reasonable probability.

Notes and References

Chapter One

1. She has received, so far, three important literary prizes: *Prix de la sélection des Libraires de France*, *Prix Fémina*, and *Prix René Julliard*.

2. One of the most widely used critical works on the anti-novel is Claude Mauriac's *The New Literature*, trans. Samuel I. Stone (New York: G. Braziller, 1959).

3. Except for quotations from works by Marguerite Duras which are available in English, all translations from French in this book are mine.

Chapter Two

1. These are the last words of Jean-Paul Sartre's play *Huis clos* (1945).

2. For this literary theme and others closely connected with it, the reader could profitably consult Germaine Brée's and Margaret Guiton's *The French Novel From Gide to Camus* (New York: Harcourt, Brace & World Inc., 1962), in particular the chapter entitled "Private Worlds."

3. In his famous article "Mauriac et la liberté," *Situations I* (Paris: Gallimard, 1947), Sartre pointed out that Mauriac's imposition of his views on his fictional characters is, in effect, prompted by a desire to propagandize. He implied that the conflict in Mauriac between the novelist and the Catholic is not solvable, and concluded that, since God is not a writer, Mauriac could not pretend to be one either.

4. Bernard Pingaud, *Ecrivains d'aujourd'hui 1940-1960* (Paris: Bernard Grasset, 1960), p. 208.

5. *Ibid.*, p. 210.

6. The dominance of the lifeless on life is, of course, a constant in contemporary literature in France and elsewhere. In this connection see my article "The Validity of Ionesco's Contempt," *The Texas Quarterly* (Winter 1963-64), pp. 137-43.

7. The analysis of tropisms is of particular interest to the New Novelists: Nathalie Sarraute's *Tropisms*, already mentioned in Chapter 1, is a case in point. I discuss the theme further in my article "The

Reader as Co-Creator in Nathalie Sarraute's Novels," *Renascence* (Summer 1964), pp. 201-18.

8. Armand Hoog, "The Itinerary of Marguerite Duras," *Yale French Studies*, XXIV (1959), pp. 68-69.

9. The phrase "all the others whom I shall never know" is repeated later by another female character, Anne-Marie Roche, of the play "La Musica"; see Chapter 5.

10. Jean-Paul Sartre's *La Nausée* appeared in 1938.

11. Germaine Brée and Margaret Guiton in *op. cit.*, pp. 207-8, speak only briefly of the possibility that Roquentin might be able to express in a book what the composer of "Some of These Days" had put into the song; but they dismiss the idea and opt for an interpretation of insanity as the only credible conclusion to the hero's impasse.

12. Albert Camus's *Le Mythe de Sisyphe* was published in 1942. While it is possible that Marguerite Duras had known of it or had read it by 1944, Camus's conclusion, "The struggle toward the summits is enough to fill the heart of man. One must imagine that Sisyphus is happy," did not seize the imagination of the public until after his other works, novels, and plays, became universally known, that is, around 1950.

13. Translated in this country under the title *The Sea Wall*; in England, as *A Sea of Troubles*. The quotations are taken from the American version.

14. Germaine Brée, "The Contemporary French Novel 1950-1960," *French Culture Today* (Summer 1961), p. 4.

15. Maurice Blanchot, *Le Livre à venir* (Paris: Gallimard, 1959), pp. 186-87.

16. "Outdoor *Snake Pit*," *Time* (March 16, 1953), pp. 118-20.

17. M. Bellasis, "Ardours and Endurances," *The Tablet* (March 28, 1953), p. 252.

18. Gérard d'Houville, "Lectures romanesques," *La Revue des deux mondes* (December 15, 1952), pp. 728-29.

19. Gaëtan Picon, *Panorama de la nouvelle littérature* (Paris: Gallimard, 1960), p. 161.

20. See above.

21. Armand Hoog, *op. cit.*, p. 69.

22. *Ibid.*, p. 69.

23. Jacques Guicharnaud, "Woman's Fate: Marguerite Duras," *Yale French Studies*, XXVII (1961), p. 106.

24. *Ibid.* p. 112.

25. The theme of evanescence recurs often in contemporary aliterature. On this subject see Eugene Ionesco, *Notes et contre-notes* (Paris: Gallimard, 1962), p. 135.

26. See Chapter 1.

27. Her abandonment to Agosti, that is her reincarnation, is prompted by the fact that he looks so much like Joseph.

28. The best-known part of Mademoiselle de Scudéry's novel *Clélie* (1654-60), representing on a map the different obstacles to be surmounted on the way to true love.

29. Which is not to say that Marguerite Duras has written, in *Un Barrage contre le Pacifique*, a story overly concerned with sexuality. This is no *Histoire d'O* (see Chapter 1, above), and in the phrase "bordering on the scandalous" the emphasis is on the first word.

30. The French is as follows: *Que dans l'amour les différences puissent s'annuler à ce point, elle ne l'oublierait plus.* It is noteworthy that the adjective *physical* has been added by the translator. It is difficult to see why, for it appears to limit the noun it modifies. At any rate, how the differences between the two lovers are nullified by Agosti's gesture remains a mystery. It is clear from the context, however, that what Suzanne feels is tenderness, or even love, momentarily, for the man whose uncommon gesture she watches in dismay.

31. Gérard d'Houville, *op. cit.*, p. 730.

32. "Floating Picnic: *The Sailor from Gibraltar*," *Time* (July 7, 1967), p. E4; anonymous.

33. Armand Hoog, *op. cit.*, pp. 70-71.

34. *Ibid.*, p. 71.

35. Anonymous, *Time, op. cit.*, p. E4.

36. *Ibid.*, p. 88.

37. *Ibid.*, p. E4.

38. Gérard d'Houville, *op. cit.*, p. 730.

39. *Ibid.*, p. 729.

40. For example, Alain Robbe-Grillet's *Dans le labyrinthe* (1959).

Chapter Three

1. Pierre de Boisdeffre, *Une Histoire vivante de la littérature d'aujourd'hui* (Paris: Librairie Académique Perrin, 1964), p. 439.

2. See below.

3. Armand Hoog, *op. cit.*, p. 71.

4. "A la recherche du roman," *Les Cahiers du Sud* (April 1956), p. 309.

5. Letter of the dramatist Alfred Jarry to his friend Jean Saltas; quoted by Leonard Cabell Pronko in *Avant-Grade, The Experimental Theater in France* (Berkeley: University of California Press, 1962), p. 6.

6. Alfred Jarry is the famous author of *Ubu roi* (1896), a prophetic play which anticipated the topsy-turvy world of the twentieth century through its unusual verve, and pointed to the absurd

theater of Ionesco, Beckett, and others through its deep-cutting social satire, grotesqueness, and exaggeration.

7. As in the beginning of each chapter; see above.

Chapter Four

1. Robert Abirached, "Marguerite Duras: *Des Journées entières dans les arbres*," *La Nouvelle Revue Française*, XXVII (1966), 345.

2. *Ibid.*, p. 345.

3. At the time of the publication of *Des Journées entières dans les arbres* the events which form the basis of her first play, *Les Viaducs de la Seine-et-Oise*, took place in France, and it is quite probable that she began thinking about the theater in 1954; see Chapter 5.

4. Extreme hunger and thirst, physical and intellectual, constitute the theme of Ionesco's celebrated play *La Soif et la faim* (1966), presented in Paris at the same time as the dramatic version of *Des Journées*.

5. An Alsatian dish of cold cuts, potatoes, and sauerkraut.

6. Yet, the paralytic characters of Beckett and the moral corpses of Ionesco differ in that their disintegration is almost always absolute.

7. Robert Abirached, *op. cit.*, p. 347.

8. Theater founded in Paris in 1797; known today as the Théâtre de France.

9. See Chapter 6, below.

10. Christine Garnier, "Revue dramatique," *La Revue des deux mondes* (February 1966), pp. 455-56.

11. Armand Hoog, *op. cit.*, p. 72.

12. Marguerite Duras had explored this theme already in *Les Petits Chevaux de Tarquinia*; see Chapter 3, Sara's decision based on the principle that leaving is no different from staying.

13. Suzanne, of *Un Barrage contre le Pacifique*.

14. See below.

15. See note 6 to Chapter 2.

16. Marguerite Duras, *Le Square* (New York: The Macmillan Company, 1965); Claude Morhange Bégué's Introduction, p. 1.

17. See below.

18. There is a similarity to be found here between the union's inability to help and the Communists' lack of support of the poor in "Madame Dodin"; see above.

19. See my article "The antitheism of Jean Genet," *The Antioch Review* (Fall 1964), pp. 387-401.

20. Claude Morhange Bégué, *op. cit.*, p. 4.

21. Jean-Paul Sartre, *Saint Genet, comédien et martyr* (Paris: Gallimard, 1952), p. 172.

22. Jean-Paul Sartre, *L'Existentialisme est un humanisme* (Paris: Nagel, 1946), pp. 46-47.

23. Claude Roy, "Sur Genet et Duras," *La Nouvelle Revue Française*, XVIII (1961), 314; the italics are the critic's.

24. Armand Hoog, *op. cit.*, pp. 72-73.

25. Marguerite Duras, *Four Novels by Marguerite Duras* (New York: Grove Press, 1965), Germaine Brée's Introduction, pp. xii-xiv.

26. Armand Hoog, *op. cit.*, p. 73.

27. *Ibid.*, p. 73.

28. John W. Kneller, "Elective Emphaties and Musical Affinities," *Yale French Studies*, XXVII (1961), p. 114.

29. *Ibid.*, p. 118.

30. Mademoiselle Giraud attempts to teach the child Anton Diabelli's *Sonatina;* a sonatina is a shorter, less pretentious sonata.

31. See Germaine Brée's Introduction to *Four Novels by Marguerite Duras*, p. xi; a concise discussion of the connection between the anti-novel and the cinema form, both dealing with "the staging of a pathetic, restrained and cleverly calculated development of a brief story," is to be found in R. M. Albérès' *Histoire du roman moderne* (Paris: Albin Michel, 1962), p. 332.

32. See Chapter 3, above.

33. See Chapter 3, above.

34. Armand Hoog, *op. cit.*, p. 73.

35. Germaine Brée's Introduction to *Four Novels by Marguerite Duras*, p. xv; R. M. Albérès, *ibid.*, pp. 332-33, points likewise to the author's cinematographic technique in this novel, as does Gérard d'Houville (see below).

36. Jacques Guicharnaud, *op. cit.*, p. 110.

37. Gérard d'Houville, "Lectures romanesques," *La Revue des deux mondes* (August 15, 1960), p. 734.

38. Germaine Brée, Introduction to *Four Novels by Marguerite Duras*, p. xv.

39. Gérard d'Houville, *La Revue des deux mondes* (August 15, 1960), p. 734.

40. John K. Simon, "Marguerite Duras' *L'Après-midi de Monsieur Andesmas*," *Books Abroad* (Autumn 1962), pp. 390-91.

41. *Ibid.*, p. 391.

42. Jacques Guicharnaud, *op. cit.*, p. 112.

43. Robert André, "Marguerite Duras: *Le Ravissement de Lol V. Stein*," *La Nouvelle revue française*, XXIV (1964), 145.

44. Kenneth S. White, "Marguerite Duras' *Le Ravissement de Lol V. Stein*," *Books Abroad* (Winter 1965), p. 42.

45. Stanley Kauffmann, "Nothing New," *The New Republic* (January 14, 1967), p. 26.

46. Nathalie Sarraute, *L'Ere du soupçon* (Paris: Gallimard, 1956), p. 31.

47. Bettina L. Knapp, "Marguerite Duras. *Le Vice-Consul*," *Books Abroad* (Autumn 1966), p. 424.

48. Kléber Haedens, "A Sleepwalker's Curry," *Atlas* (April 1966), p. 254.

49. As early as 1925 André Gide wrote *Les Faux monnayeurs,* and numerous other examples exist.

50. Bettina L. Knapp, *op. cit.,* p. 424.

51. Kléber Haedens, *op. cit.,* p. 255.

52. André Thérive, "Marguerite Duras: *Le Vice-Consul*," *La Revue des deux mondes* (July 1, 1966), p. 116.

53. *Ibid.,* p. 115.

54. Bettina L. Knapp, *op. cit.,* p. 424.

55. See Chapter 1, above.

Chapter Five

1. For a detailed description of "total theater" see Antonin Artaud's *Le Théâtre et son double* (Paris: Gallimard, 1938).

2. Michel Corvin's *Le Théâtre nouveau en France* (Paris: P.U.F., 1963) is a useful book on the contemporary French theater; I know of no work in English that can be of so much help to the non-specialist as Corvin's.

3. See Martin Esslin's *The Theater of the Absurd* (Garden City, New York: Anchor Books, 1961); also Leonard Cabell Pronko's *Avant-Garde: The Experimental Theater in France* (Berkeley: University of California Press, 1962).

4. Samuel Beckett, *Textes pour rien* (Paris: Editions de Minuit, 1955), p. 101.

5. Willis H. Bowen, "Marguerite Duras: *Théâtre I*," *Books Abroad* (Winter 1967), p. 56.

6. In the last line of the poem "Le Voyage" in the collection *Les Fleurs du mal* (1857).

7. Poirot-Delpech, *Le Monde* (November 14, 1965), p. 17.

8. Willis H. Bowen, *op. cit.,* p. 101.

9. *Ibid.,* p. 101.

10. See Chronology.

11. Jacques Lemarchand, "Les Deux erreurs présomptueuses de Marguerite Duras," *Le Figaro Littéraire* (January 15-21, 1968), p. 34.

12. *Ibid.,* p. 34.

13. Quoted by Jacques Lemarchand, *ibid.,* p. 34; source not given.

14. Jean Giraudoux's *La Folle de Chaillot* (1945) is perhaps the most outstanding example of the century so far.

15, Reine-Marie Desnues, "Marguerite Duras," *Christiane* (March 1969), p. 14.

16. *Ibid.*, p. 14.

Chapter Six

1. Marguerite Duras, *Hiroshima, mon amour* (New York: Grove Press, 1961), p. 13.

2. *Ibid.*, p. 12.

3. *Ibid.*, p. 112.

4. *Ibid.*, p. 10.

5. See above, note 2.

6. Maryvonne Butcher, *"Hiroshima, mon amour* by Marguerite Duras," *The Tablet* (March 18, 1961), p. 258.

7. Gérard Jarlot has become known for his three novels: *Les Armes blanches* (1946), *Un Mauvais lieu* (1948), and *Le Périple d'Autun* (1953).

8. Marguerite Duras, *Hiroshima, mon amour,* p. 7.

9. The hobo, as a character encountered frequently in contemporary literature, has been alluded to before: see Chapter 3, above.

10. Especially in *Dix heures et demie du soir en été.*

Selected Bibliography

PRIMARY SOURCES

Les Impudents. Paris: Plon, 1943.

La Vie tranquille. Paris: Gallimard, 1944.

Un Barrage contre le Pacifique. Paris: Gallimard, 1950. *The Sea Wall*. Tr. by Herma Briffault. New York: Pellegrini & Cudahy, 1952.

Le Marin de Gibraltar. Paris: Gallimard, 1952. *The Sailor From Gibraltar*. Tr. by Barbara Grey. London: Calder & Boyars, 1966.

Les Petits Chevaux de Tarquinia. Paris: Gallimard, 1953.

Des Journées entières dans les arbres. Paris: Gallimard, 1954.

Le Square. Paris: Gallimard, 1955. *The Square*. Tr. by Sonia Pitt-Rivers & Irina Morduch. In *Four Novels by Marguerite Duras*, New York: Grove Press, 1965.

Moderato cantabile. Paris: Editions de Minuit, 1958. *Moderato Cantabile*. Tr. by Richard Seaver. In *Four Novels by Marguerite Duras*, New York: Grove Press, 1965.

Les Viaducs de la Seine-et-Oise. Paris: Gallimard, 1960.

Hiroshima, mon amour. Paris: Gallimard, 1960. *Hiroshima, mon amour*. Tr. by Richard Seaver. New York: Grove Press, 1961.

Dix heures et demie du soir en été. Paris: Gallimard, 1960. *10:30 on a Summer Night*. Tr. by Anne Borchardt. In *Four Novels by Marguerite Duras*, New York: Grove Press, 1965.

Une Aussi longue absence in collaboration with Gérard Jarlot. Paris: Gallimard, 1961.

L'Après-midi de Monsieur Andesmas. Paris: Gallimard, 1962. *The Afternoon of Mr. Andesmas*. Tr. by Anne Borchardt. In *Four Novels by Marguerite Duras*, New York: Grove Press, 1965.

Le Ravissement de Lol V. Stein. Paris: Gallimard, 1964. *The Ravishing of Lol V. Stein*. Tr. by Richard Seaver. New York: Grove Press, 1966.

Théâtre I ("Les Eaux et forêts," "Le Square," "La Musica"). Paris: Gallimard, 1965.

Le Vice-Consul. Paris: Gallimard, 1966.

L'Amante anglaise. Paris: Gallimard, 1967. *L'Amante Anglaise*. Tr. by Barbara Grey. London: H. Hamilton, 1969.

Théâtre II (*Suzanna Andler, Des Journées entières dans les arbres*,

"Yes, peut-être," "Le Shaga," *Un Homme est venu me voir*). Paris: Gallimard, 1968.
Détruire dit-elle. Paris. Editions de Minuit, 1969.

SECONDARY SOURCES

(Footnote entries which do not refer directly to Marguerite Duras' works and those which are not considered especially useful as background material have been omitted from this listing.)

ABIRACHED, ROBERT. "Marguerite Duras: *Des Journées entières dans les arbres*," *La Nouvelle Revue Française*, XXVII (1966), 345-47. Enlightening review of the play version of *Des Journées*, useful for a better understanding of the short story.

ALBÉRÈS, ROBERT M. *Histoire du roman moderne.* Paris: Albin Michel, 1952. A background work, perhaps a little difficult for the non-specialist.

ANDRÉ, ROBERT. "Marguerite Duras: *Le Ravissement de Lol V. Stein*," *La Nouvelle Revue Française*, XXIV (1964), 144-45. Brief review of the novel, but one of the very few commentaries which exists.

ANONYMOUS. "Floating Picnic: The Sailor from Gilbraltar," *Time* (July 7, 1967), p. E4. A very scant review of the novel.

————. "Outdoor *Snake Pit*," *Time* (March 16, 1953), pp. 118-20. A rather inimical view of Marguerite Duras' early works.

ARTAUD, ANTONIN. *Le Théâtre et son double.* Paris: Gallimard, 1938. Essential for an understanding of contemporary theater.

BÉGUÉ, CLAUDE MORHANGE. *Marguerite Duras: Le Square.* New York: The Macmillan Co., 1965. Excellent introduction to a college edition of *Le Square*.

BELLASIS, M. "Ardours and Endurances," *The Tablet* (March 28, 1953), p. 252. A representation of the cool reception given in England to *Un Barrage contre le Pacifique*.

BLANCHOT, MAURICE. *Le Livre à venir.* Paris: Gallimard, 1958. A useful book for the background to the contemporary novel.

BOISDEFFRE, PIERRE DE. *Une Histoire vivante de la littérature d'aujourd'hui.* Paris: Librairie Académique Perrin, 1964. A critical work of monumental proportions clearly living up to its title.

BOWEN, WILLIS H. "Marguerite Duras: *Théâtre I*," *Books Abroad* (Winter 1967), p. 56. A poor, uniformed review of *Théâtre I*.

BRÉE, GERMAINE. "The Contemporary French Novel 1950-1960," *French Culture Today* (Summer 1961), pp. 1-6. Short article on several major French writers of the period stated, including Madame Duras.

————. The Introduction to *Four Novels by Marguerite Duras.* New York: Grove Press, 1965. Clear, concise analysis of *The Square*,

Moderato Cantabile, 10:30 on a Summer Night and *The Afternoon of Mr. Andesmas.*

BRÉE, GERMAINE and GUITON, MARGARET. *The French Novel From Gide to Camus.* New York: Harcourt, Brace & World Inc., 1962. An introductory work, useful for its chapter entitled "Private Worlds."

BUTCHER, MARYVONNE. "*Hiroshima, mon amour* by Marguerite Duras," *The Tablet* (March 18, 1961), pp. 256-58. A penetrating review of the first Durasian film.

CORVIN, MICHEL. *Le Théâtre nouveau en France.* Paris: P.U.F., 1963. In my opinion, the best introductory book on the contemporary French theater.

DELPECH-POIROT. Review of *La Musica, Le Monde* (November 14, 1965), p. 17. A thorough appreciation of the play.

DESNUES, REINE-MARIE. "Marguerite Duras," *Christiane* (March 1969), pp. 13-15. An introduction to Madame Duras' works for the French Canadian public.

ESSLIN, MARTIN. *The Theater of the Absurd.* Garden City, New York: Anchor Books, 1961. Contains important elucidations on trends and dramatists of twentieth-century theater.

GARNIER, CHRISTINE. "Revue dramatique," *La Revue des deux mondes* (February 1966), pp. 455-56. Brief review of the play version of *Des Journées.*

GUICHARNAUD, JACQUES. "Woman's Fate: Marguerite Duras," *Yale French Studies*, XXVII (1961), pp. 106-13. A revealing article on several of Madame Duras' works, particularly helpful for an understanding of her female characters.

HAEDENS, KLÉBER. "A Sleepwalker's Curry," *Atlas* (April 1966), pp. 254-55. A conservative's point of view on Madame Duras in general and on *Le Vice-Consul* in particular; unfriendly, incorrect, even rash.

HOOG, ARMAND. "The Itinerary of Marguerite Duras," *Yale French Studies*, XXIV (1959), 68-73. A study of some of the early novels, somewhat critical of *Le Square* and the emerging anti-novel vein of the author.

HOUVILLE, GÉRARD D'. "Lectures romanesques," *La Revue des deux mondes* (December 15, 1952), pp. 728-30. Short review of *Un Barrage contre le Pacifique.*

————. "Lectures romanesques," *La Revue des deux mondes* (August 15, 1960), pp. 733-34. Excellent review of *Dix heures et demie du soir en été,* especially for an understanding of the cinematographic technique of the writer.

IONESCO, EUGÈNE. *Notes et contre-notes.* Paris: Gallimard, 1962.

Contains indispensable comments on contemporary theater; it is very readable and very intriguing.

KAUFFMANN, STANLEY. "Nothing New," *The New Republic* (January 14, 1967), p. 26. Scant review of *Le Ravissement de Lol V. Stein.*

KNAPP, BETTINA L. "Marguerite Duras: *Le Vice-Consul,*" *Books Abroad* (Autumn 1966), p. 424. Brief but sensitive and penetrating review of the novel.

KNELLER, JOHN W. "Elective Emphaties and Musical Affinities," *Yale French Studies,* XXVII (1961), 114-19. Perhaps the best commentary on *Moderato cantabile.*

LEMARCHAND, JACQUES. "Les Deux erreurs présomptueuses de Marguerite Duras," *Le Figaro Littéraire* (January 15-21, 1968), p. 34. An extremely critical review of "Yes, peut-être" and "Le Shaga."

MAURICE, CLAUDE. *The New Literature.* Tr. by Samuel I. Stone. New York: G. Braziller, 1959. An excellent examination of aliterature's beginnings and trends, widely used, profound insights; translation is awkward in spots.

PICON, GAËTAN. *Panorama de la nouvelle littérature.* Paris: Gallimard, 1960. Contains significant background material to contemporary literature.

PINGAUD, BERNARD. *Ecrivains d'aujourd'hui.* Paris: Bernard Grasset, 1960. Devotes a chapter to each of the major and not so major contemporary French writers; succinct summaries, should be used only by those at least partly familiar with the authors included.

PRONKO, LEONARD CABELL. *Avant-Garde: The Experimental Theater in France.* Berkeley: University of California Press, 1962. There is nothing on Marguerite Duras here, but there is a great deal on Ionesco and Beckett. A necessary background work for students of contemporary theater.

ROY, CLAUDE. "Sur Genet et Duras," *La Nouvelle Revue Française,* XVIII (1961), 313-15. The best review I have seen on the play version of *Le Square.*

SIMON, JOHN K. "Marguerite Duras: *L'Après-midi de Monsieur Andesmas,*" *Books Abroad* (Autumn 1962), pp. 390-91. Very brief review of the novel, critical of the Durasian allegedly coy style.

THÉRIVE, ANDRÉ. "Marguerite Duras: *Le Vice-Consul,*" *La Revue des deux mondes* (July 1, 1966), pp. 115-17. Another conservative's view of the novel; makes sweeping, uncorroborated allegations disparaging to Marguerite Duras.

WHITE, KENNETH S. "Marguerite Duras: *Le Ravissement de Lol V. Stein,*" *Books Abroad* (Winter 1965), p. 42. Scant but appreciative review of the novel.

Index

Adamov, Arthur, 57, 58; *L'Invasion*, 58; *La Parodie*, 58; *Le Professeur Teranne*, 58; *Théâtre I*, 58
André, Robert, 108
Anouilh, Jean, 141; *Joan of Arc*, 141; *Antigone*, 141
Aymé, Marcel, 56; *Les Mauvais coups*, 56; *Uranus*, 56

Barrault, Jean-Louis, 64, 117
Baudelaire, Charles, 129
Beauvoir, Simone de, 14, 15, 16, 17, 19, 52, 118, 156; *Le Deuxième sexe*, 16; *Mémoires d'une jeune fille rangée*, 16
Beckett, Samuel, 18, 57, 58, 66, 77, 81, 100, 121; *Malone Dies*, 57; *Molloy*, 57; *The Unnameable*, 57; *Waiting for Godot*, 57
Bégué, Claude Morhange, 84
Bernanos, Georges, 27
Blanchot, Maurice, 35
Blin, Roger, 117
Boisdeffre, Pierre de, 55; *Histoire vivante de la littérature d'aujourd' hui*, 55
Bowen, W. H., 131
Brecht, Bertolt, 118
Brée, Germaine, 35, 87, 95, 99
Butcher, Maryvonne, 149
Butor, Michel, 18

Les Cahiers du Sud, 56
Caldwell, Erskine, 31; *God's Little Acre*, 31; *Tobacco Road*, 31
Camus, Albert, 15, 156; *L'Exil et le royaume*, 15; *Myth of Sisyphus*, 34
Cannes Film Festival, 145, 150
La Carte de Tendre, 42
Cayrol, Jean, 58; *Le vivrai l'amour des autres*, 58

Colette, 13; *Gigi*, 13
Corneille, Pierre, 117
Curtis, Jean-Louis, 56; *Les Forêts de la nuit*, 56; *Les Justes causes*, 56

Descartes, René, 77
Donne, John, 57
Duras, Marguerite, position in French letters of today, 17-19, 154-56; summary of participation in American-type novel, 53-54; summary of participation in the Anti-Novel, 116; as playwright, 131, 143-44; as scenario writer, 153

WRITINGS OF:
L'Amante anglaise, 112, 131
L'Après-midi de Monsieur Andesmas, 18, 100-108, 116, 154
"Le Boa," 64, 71-75, 78
"Les Chantiers," 64, 78-82, 101, 102, 116, 154
Dix heures et demie du soir en été, 18, 95-100, 107, 153
"Les Eaux et forêts," 123-26, 131, 140, 155
Hiroshima, mon amour, 67, 82, 145-49, 150, 153, 155, 156
Les Impudents, 17, 20-28, 33, 41, 44, 53, 108
Des Journées entières dans les arbres, 55, 64-71, 78, 82, 94, 131, 134, 143
"Madame Dodin," 64, 75-78, 136
Le Marin de Gibraltar, 17, 39, 46-53, 59, 151, 153
Moderato cantabile, 18, 88-

169